# THE BURIED BARONY

D1627315

## BY THE SAME AUTHOR

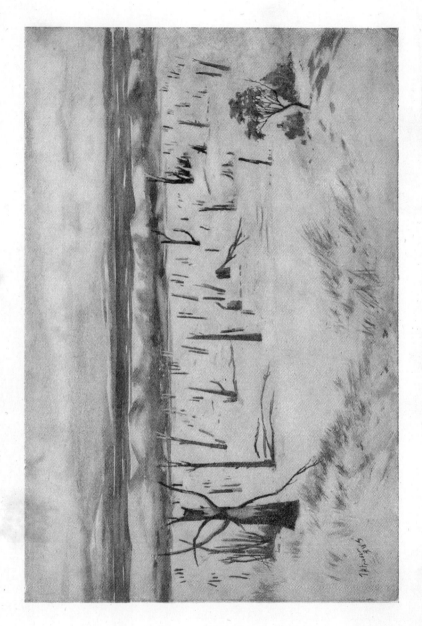

The Culbin Sands and Moray Firth

ALASDAIR ALPIN MACGREGOR

# THE
# BURIED BARONY

*With a frontispiece from a painting by*
*Mrs. R. G. Fraser, and 54 illustrations*
*mostly from photographs by the Author*

LONDON
ROBERT HALE LIMITED
18 Bedford Square W.C. 1

*First Published in* 1949

Printed in Great Britain
by T. and A. CONSTABLE LTD., Hopetoun Street,
Printers to the University of Edinburgh

# DEDICATION

ROBERT CHRISTIE

1868-1946

&

ELIZABETH TAYLOR

HIS SPOUSE

1863-1945

MY DEAR ROBERT & LEESBETH,

Time, in its inexorable passage, has now bereft us of you both.
When you wrote me, Robert, at the onset of last winter, that
Leesbeth was tranquil and beautiful in her serenity, but that the
vital spark in her was so feeble that at any moment she might
have slipped away from us, I little thought the ensuing Hogmanay
was to see the last of her, and that so soon thereafter she would
be lying in her narrow cell at Kirk-Yetholm, among her kindred
there.

Under what benign guidance did I first find my way to Kirk-
Yetholm, that summer's day I espied you seated in sunlight by
your doorstep, on the fringe of the village green? I wonder,
Robert, whether you recollect that first meeting as vividly as I
do! We were deep in conversation about Queen Esther Faa and
her Romany tribe, when Leesbeth (and she so couthie, so gentle
of tongue) came to the door and, in a whisper, said: "Robert,
are ye no' takin' yer freend in for a moothfu' o' tea?" That
invitation was the prelude to one of my most cherished friendships. It brought me back to Yetholm year after year. As for
you, dear Leesbeth, I hardly suppose you will mind if I now
confess that, at first sight, you instantly reminded me of one
about whom I had been reading a day or two before—the spouse
of Adam Weir of Hermiston, yon "dwaibly body frae the first".
It was the fragile in you that attracted me; and, when I return

v

to Kirk-Yetholm, I shall miss the touch of your sensitive hand, and the endearing cadence of your voice.

As for you, Robert, you had stepped straight out of *The Waverley Novels*, and were to be seated just where it was destined I should find you.

It is but a few weeks since you welcomed "the Kelso Laddie", when, once again, after the lapse of those years of war, he and his supporters rode into Yetholm in ancient Border fashion. Your speech on that occasion was epic. I can well imagine the laughter and applause it stimulated. "*In the name of all here assembled, I bid you a hearty welcome, full of warmth and good feeling; and in so doing I fall back upon a Border expression (though I must reverse it to suit the occasion) that you have managed to come 'Safe In'. We here and now give you the assurance, the guarantee, that we will see to it that you get 'Safe Oot'!*"

You entertained them as you so often entertained me, from your lair by the cheek o' the fire, while toving at the pipe. (You see, the auld Scots words and sayings, which stuck to you as do bur-thistles, now stick to me in like manner!)

Do you remember the account you once gave Louise and me of the coronation of King Charlie Blythe? Do you recall how, after one of our Border excursions in my car, you took me a-wandering in imagination over the Lomond Hills you knew in boyhood? Do you recall the visit we paid to those queer folk at Hazeldean, or, better still, the day we went to Kalemouth to see the Gordons?—"The Twa Doos", you always called them—"now of 13, Spottiswoode Street, Edinburgh", as you have reminded me in innumerable letters since that most agreeable sojourn with them at Kalemouth. What a lovely and loving couple they are! Did wayfarers ever find, at the end of their journey, so fervent a welcome, so delectable a spread?

But surely the most memorable of all our jaunts were those we made to Flodden Field, by way of Mindrum Mill, so close at hand. I remember particularly our travelling there one day in May, when the hedgerows were drooping white with hawthorn, and the craggy outcroppings of the Cheviots were splashed with the gold of gorse. I remember, too, a day in June—a gey gusty day it was!—when the roadside rocked with white hemlock and sheaves of wild geranium, when the meadows of the Borderland rippled and undulated before the wind's passage, like waves upon some inland lake, when ringed pigeons hurried overhead, and baby rabbits scurried to their hidie-holes among the lengthening grass. On alighting, we ascended those wooden steps leading us through a hedge into a corn-field. Thereafter we climbed a steep path to the spot whereon stands the monument:

## FLODDEN

### 1513

## TO THE BRAVE OF BOTH NATIONS

### ERECTED 1910

"What touched you yonder, now?" you asked me on leaving that corn-field, knowing full well that we were of one mind. "To the Brave of Both Nations—in good taste! Ay, in good taste!" you remarked. "No venom yonder, no ill-feeling. . . . But the puir Scots had a lang way tae carry their deid for burial in consecrated ground at Kirk-Yetholm. I wudna hae likit the job!"

The old house by the Green o' Kirk-Yetholm will be quieter now, and sad. Not that it was ever anything but quiet. Therein resided much of its charm. Its silence in the mornings, when one heard so plainly the crow of cock at some farmyard in the Vale of Bowmont, or the bleat of lamb among the Cheviot fells, near at hand, became accentuated when you, Robert, rose and shook your feathers. That was, indeed, a stirring flutter you gave in response to Peggy's announcing that she had dished the porridge!

It lies uncomfortably on my conscience that I did not come your way when in Scotland in the autumn. I now learn that you were breathing your last in the Royal Infirmary of Edinburgh just as *The Flying Scotsman* was hurrying me southward across the Border. This is greatly grievous to me, for, when travelling through Berwick (which I supposed to be the nearest point to you) I pictured your waiting for me in the Square at Kelso— "Kelsae, Bonnie Kelsae"—and escorting me, as of yore, to your local bus, which even *I* had got to know quite intimately. Peggy writes, however, that I must return to the Borderland as though Leesbeth and you were still there to greet me, and that there will aye be the scone in the press. In winter, when the frost, as you once remarked, freezes the very frost, I may go back to Kirk-Yetholm. Or, perhaps, I may defer until the time of the Teuchat Storm, the Peesweeps' Blast. Yet, back to these haunts of yours I shall assuredly go, for memories' sake, and for a blaw o' Cheviot air.

To think that one might lie in the kirkyard of so sweet a place might almost make one happy in contemplating Death's irrevocable decree. Your Cheviot sward is comforting: it enshrines the evergreen of remembrance.

In sincerity,

ALASDAIR.

# CONTENTS

# ILLUSTRATIONS

xi

## Spanish Gold

## The Sea-Dogs of Scotland

## Gypsies of the Borderland

# ILLUSTRATIONS

## Rothiemurchus : An Ancient Highland Heritage

## Covenanters' Conventicle—1666-1945

# PREFACE

In this age of speedy travel, it is surprising how little is known about the less accessible parts even of a relatively small country like Scotland. The purport of this volume, then, is to introduce something fresh and novel about a land, the charm and interest of which are unlimited.

Abridged versions of Chapters One, Two, Four, and Five have appeared in the *Quarterly Review, Chambers's Journal, Geographical Magazine*, and the *Cornhill*. To the Editors of these, formal acknowledgment is made for permission to reprint. To J. N. Steers, Esq., St. Catherine's College, Cambridge, and to the proprietors of the *Aberdeen Bon Accord & Northern Pictorial* I am indebted for their generosity in having supplemented the illustrations accompanying our opening chapter.

Alasdair Alpin MacGregor

London,
1949.

# CHAPTER ONE

## THE BURIED BARONY

IS it possible to wrest a dividend from a desert?

To this question the answer may well be in the affirmative, when we consider the attempts that in recent years have been made to reclaim the vast and fertile tracts now buried beneath the great sand-hills known as the Culbin Sands, and to retrieve something at least of the fortunes of the Buried Barony. Here, indeed, is a Scottish desert that even yet may rejoice and blossom.

The Culbin Sands are situated in the parish of Dyke, in the county of Moray. On the north and west they are bounded by the sandy shores of the Moray Firth. On the east they border that flat, spacious basin of tide-swept sand known as Findhorn Bay, through which the river of the same name, rising among the fastnesses of the Monadhliath, many miles to the southward, flows by diverse and ever-changing channels to meet the sea. On the south they march with the historic Laich-lands of Moray— the name applied in olden times, and even at the present day, to the extensive farmlands, which are reputed to be among the most fertile in the British Isles. In fact, Culbin itself once constituted the most productive part of the Laich. To-day, however, Culbin is the only region in Britain where sand-dunes and shifting sand-hills occupy an area sufficiently large to create the impression that they comprise an arid, lifeless desert.

The tragedy of Culbin might be compared with the fate that overtook ash-smothered Pompeii. It is a tragedy of which at least something is known to everyone interested in Scotland. Literally in a night, it is said, a smiling estate supporting a flourishing and industrious community was overwhelmed by a great storm of sea-sand driven before an unrelenting gale from the west. Historic records show, of course, that the whole of the low country of Moray was deluged by the sea during the eleventh century, and that, early in the twelfth, successive sand-storms already were beginning to make serious encroachments on the prosperous Barony of Culbin. But it was not until the autumn of 1694 that the final catastrophe engulfed Culbin, rendering it

A
I

not merely one of the most barren regions of Scotland, but one of Scotland's most eerie phenomena. According to tradition still current in Moray, the great sand-storm of that autumn broke so unexpectedly that harvesters were obliged to abandon their scythes in the corn-fields. As the dwellers on Culbin sought refuge from this catastrophe, their homes and farmlands were being smothered in waves of sand before their very eyes. It is true that a lull in the storm engendered the hope that the calamity visiting the Barony was of a temporary nature, and that the damage done alike to field and orchard, farm and dwelling-place, was not irreparable. But, when the gales resumed with their previous fury, and the delta of the Findhorn itself became choked by drifting mountains of sand, this hope was abandoned forever.

The inhabitants were distressed and mystified. They sought to explain the calamity as a curse that had come upon them from Heaven. Some regarded it as a judgment upon them for having harboured smugglers among the sand-dunes by the coast, which, up till that time at any rate, had shown no indication that they might engulf them : some put the blame on the Baron of Culbin for the scant respect in which he held the Fourth Commandment : some were of opinion that the Baron's card-playing with the Devil Himself was the cause of their doom.

To-day Culbin lies beneath the desert ; and the immediate activities of man are more concerned with fixing the sands and preventing further drifting than with restoring to the Barony its pristine glories.

The sand-storm of 1694 did not confine its devastating hand solely to Culbin. Gradually the sands drifted eastward and landward, forming numerous mounds in their journey. They still lie to a fair depth upon stretches of the parishes of Kinloss and Duffus. Evidences of this sand-storm are also to be seen in the northern parts of the neighbouring parish of Alves, where its loamy character is believed to have added appreciably to the fertility of the soil.

\* \* \* \* \*

Whence came all this sand ? The answer is to be found in the fact that, through natural causes, and to an exceptional degree, considerable stretches of the shore of the Moray Firth in this

locality have been favourable to the accumulation of sand, and to
the formation of giant sand-hills. To begin with, the Findhorn
for centuries has been carrying down great quantities of sand, and
depositing them all along this coast-line, particularly at the
points where, at different periods in its history, it has entered the
sea. Historical records as well as geological research show that
the Findhorn's course near its mouth has been as wayward as that
of its neighbour, the destructive and erratic Spey. And it has
been well established that the vast shingle deposits and swampy
areas scattered about the Culbin, many of them a considerable
distance from the Findhorn's present course, once formed part
of that river's bed. Since the currents along the impinging shores
of the Moray Firth run from east to west, sand-dunes and sand-
hills and great bars of sand have tended to accumulate to the west
of the Findhorn and of Findhorn Bay. Sand-hills of considerable
dimensions are still to be found as far west as Maviston; and the
long Bar lying offshore in this region, and stretching visibly for
a distance of at least four miles, would seem to indicate that the
sand-dunes of Maviston are small to-day in comparison with
what they were about the time that the Barony of Culbin was
overwhelmed.

In order to obtain some conception of the magnitude of
the calamity that devastated this countryside, let us look at
the estate of Culbin in its heyday—that is to say, about 250 years
ago. At that time its area was estimated roughly at 3,500 acres.
It was regarded as one of the most productive estates not merely
in Moray, but in all Scotland. It embraced sixteen fair-sized
farms, including the home-farm, which for generations was
occupied by the ancient family of Kinnaird, to whom we shall
refer later. Each tenant-farmer paid to the Baron a yearly rent
in money of two hundred pounds Scots, together with forty
bolls of wheat, bere, oats, and oatmeal, in kind. Besides these
well-favoured farms, there were numerous crofts, tenanted by
families deriving a goodly proportion of their livelihood by fishing the Findhorn and the more remunerative grounds of the
Moray Firth. So fertile was the soil, owing to the rich, alluvial
deposits brought down by the floods of the Findhorn throughout
the centuries, and so mild and equable the climate, that, when
the crops of other regions were ruined, either by prolonged

drought or by untimely frosts, the lands of the Barony of Culbin were yielding a bountiful harvest, and its orchards more fruit than the inhabitants could consume. It was one of the boasts of its husbandmen that one year an unusually heavy crop of barley was reaped, albeit not a drop of rain had fallen since before it was sown. In addition to this, the estate possessed lucrative salmon-fishings.

In 1694—the year of Culbin's burial—the rental of the estate was 2,720 pounds Scots, 640 bolls of wheat, 640 bolls of bere, 640 bolls of oats, and 640 bolls of oatmeal. When the value of the salmon-fishings was added to this, the total rental reached a value in the neighbourhood of £6,000 Scots. Little wonder, then, that in olden times the Barony of Culbin was known throughout the land as the 'Girnel', or Granary, of Moray! The Province of Moray in olden days comprised the counties of Elgin and Nairn, a portion of the county of Banff, and the greater part of what we now know as Inverness-shire.

In keeping with the income of the Barony was the mansion of Culbin, a large, square building of dressed stone, situated in the centre of the demesne amid lawns and gardens and orchards, and once the residence of the Kinnairds, who became Lairds of Culbin about the middle of the fifteenth century. The Kinnairds hailed from Perthshire. In 1440 Thomas Kinnaird of that Ilk married Giles, or Egidia, heiress of the line of Walter de Moravia, a family Flemish in origin. Walter (sometimes referred to in old records as Richard de Moravia de Culbin) is regarded as having been the first proprietor of the Culbin. On the death of Giles Kinnaird's father, her eldest son came into possession of the Perthshire estates. To the second son, Giles bequeathed her estates in Moray. In 1460 he obtained a charter of confirmation; and from that year until 1698 the lands and Barony of Culbin remained in the possession of the Kinnairds. No longer is the name of Kinnaird to be found among the county families of Moray. With the ruin of their heritage toward the close of the seventeenth century, they disappear completely from local history.

That Culbin supported a fair population is proved by documents contemporaneous with its prosperity. We know for certain that the Barony had its own place of public worship. To this day the site, beneath which it is supposed to lie, is called the Chapel Hill. Furthermore, in right of its barony, the Culbin lands were empowered to carry the dovecot that stood on a knoll hard by the mansion-house. In short, to quote Sheriff Rampini (1897), "nothing that could conduce to the comfort and convenience of the lairds of 'Coubine' was wanting".

For the Kinnairds, however, the destruction of their lands spelt complete ruin. Threatened incursions by sand had given them cause for alarm a few years earlier; and they had not altogether forgotten the serious inroads made in 1676. With their lives, but with their means of livelihood gone, the young laird, Alexander Kinnaird, together with his wife and children, escaped the sand-drifts. On July, 17th, 1695, almost a year after this astonishing superinduction of sand had desolated his fertile and populous Barony, we find the said Alexander petitioning Parliament to exempt him from the payment of cess on the pretext "that the best two parts of his estate of Culbin, by an unavoidable fatality, was quite ruined and destroyed, occasioned by great and vast heaps of sand (which had overblown the same), so that there was not a vestige to be seen of his manor-place of Culbin, yards, orchards, and mains thereof, and which within these twenty years were as considerable as many within the County of Moray".

Kinnaird succeeded in obtaining the relief he asked; and, as an expression of sympathy for him, Parliament passed the Act still on the Statute Book, prohibiting, under severe penalties, the pulling of bent, broom, or juniper bushes on the sand-hills and by the coast at Culbin and elsewhere, believing that the reckless pulling of such plants had contributed to the facility with which the wind-borne sands from the adjoining sand-dunes had drifted in great banks to overwhelm this ancient Barony. But matters became so serious for the laird and his family that a couple of years later he felt constrained to apply to the court for personal protection against his creditors, on the plea that three-fourths of his estate were irretrievably overblown with sand, and that already the remaining fourth had been sold to enable him to meet what debts he could. In the following year (1698) he disposed of a portion of his estates to a certain Alexander Duff of Drummuir, "with my goodwill and blessing". A few months later, both he and his wife were dead. An old servant of the family took charge of their infant son, and brought him to Edinburgh. There she strove to make a livelihood by needle-work both for him and for herself. When the boy came to adolescence, he enlisted in the army. Some little time thereafter he was identified by his mother's half-brother, a certain Colonel Alexander Ross, who was instrumental in procuring a commission for him. In 1743 he died without issue, having attained the rank of captain.

\*     \*     \*     \*     \*

Perhaps the most vivid account of the fate that befell Culbin is that written by George Bain, entitled *The Culbin Sands, or the Story of a Buried Estate*. Bain was editor of the *Nairnshire Telegraph*, and an authority on all matters relating to the Culbin. Though the old coast-line of the Moray Firth had been breaking up gradually, and the sand-hills in the Maviston area, some three or four miles to the west, had been encroaching slowly, but surely, on the Culbin lands and hereditaments for several years, the final catastrophe came suddenly and without warning, for-ever concealing them from sight, and leaving the inhabitants no means of ascertaining even approximately where their buried homesteads lay. According to Bain, a man ploughing had to desert his plough in the middle of the furrow. Part of this very plough, I believe, was recovered afterwards, and is now on view in the museum at Elgin, the county town of Moray. A native in process of reaping a field of late barley had to abandon his efforts. In an hour or two, plough and barley lay beneath several tons of sand. With the force as of a mighty river, the sand-drift advanced steadily and irresistibly, ruthlessly encompassing field after field. Every object obstructing its progress became the nucleus of a sand-dune. Trees veritably became the nuclei of sand-hills. Violent blasts of wind bore the sand amid the dwell-ings of the people, respecting neither the cot of the cottar nor the mansion of the laird. "In the morning", continues Bain, "after the first night of drift, the people had to break through the backs of their houses to get out. They relieved the cattle, and drove them to a place of safety. A lull in the storm succeeded, and they began to think they might still have their dwelling-houses, though their lands were ruined for ever. But the storm began again with renewed violence, and they had to flee for their lives, taking with them only such things as they could carry. What a strange scene it must have been!—these poor people rushing from their hearths and homes amidst the blinding and bewildering sand-storm. And, to add to the horror of the scene, the sand had choked the mouth of the Findhorn, which now poured its flooded waters amongst the fields and homesteads, accumulating in lakes and pools till it rose to a height by which it was able to burst the barrier to the north, and find its new outlet to the sea, in its course sweeping to destruction the old village of Findhorn, which had but a short time before been abandoned by the villagers. On returning, the people of Culbin were spellbound. . . ."

Not a trace of their homes was to be found. A desert of sand-hills, dunes, and sand-banks now covered the orchards and fertile farmlands. A great and prosperous demesne lay buried irretrievably.

Several of the tenants are said to have lingered in their old abodes, never quite relinquishing the hope that the winds would abate, and the progress of the sand be arrested. In their endeavour to remain, they strove incessantly to keep their doorways clear of sand-drifts. But eventually the accumulation became too great for them. Even their recourse to breaking through the back walls of their houses gave them but temporary respite, since the sand was soon overtopping the very roofs and chimneys, and swirling perilously around them with every wind that blew.[1]

\* \* \* \* \*

Nevertheless, traces of the Buried Barony have appeared and again *dis*-appeared from time to time. Somewhere about 1800 another furious drifting of sand, lasting for several successive days, completely altered the altitudes and contours of the sand-

[1] Dramatic and picturesque as is George Bain's account, and consistent as it may be with the popular belief that all this happened in a single night, scientific experiment has demonstrated that no sand-storm, however violent, could possibly have devastated this region in so short a space of time. Any given wind can transport only a certain weight of sand in a given time. Though, doubtless, a storm of unusual severity did occur in 1694, the wind of that year is accredited with a power which, in the light of recent calculations, is fantastic. The more acceptable explanation is, I think, that there blew in the autumn of 1694 a gale, which lasted for several days and nights, and which simply extended irreparably the damage done by the previous great sand-storm of 1676.

hills, and laid bare much of the mansion-house already concealed in the heart of one of the sand-hills for well over a century. While it remained exposed, the people of the neighbourhood proceeded to carry away, for building purposes elsewhere, many of the substantial and finely dressed stones of which it was constructed. But scarcely had they begun their dismantling operations when the winds arose, and once more smothered it in fathoms of sand.

One of the chimney-tops of the mansion was seen rising above the sand at a later date. And local tradition has it that, when a cottar living in the vicinity scrambled up the sand-hill, and shouted down the open chimney, he fled in terror when a ghostly voice answered him from within! This chimney-top remained visible for several days; and it is said that many people travelled expressly to Culbin for a sight of it. But one night the sand began to drift again; and by the morning the chimney-top had vanished completely. Toward the close of last century there was living in the locality a native who remembered having seen the walls and some other parts of a house that the wind had uncovered some forty years earlier. According to his account, the walls were formed entirely of a firm clay turf, which had been cut carefully, and placed in position with remarkable precision. A few wooden supports, in process of rapid decay, were also observed. Examination of the floor showed it to have been causewayed with rounded stones taken from an adjoining beach. Over this was a layer of clay, some four inches thick. Beating sand had worn the exposed part of the building in such a way as to give the impression of a surface engraved, or perhaps embossed. Not since then has a vestige of the old house of Culbin made its appearance. The sand-hills and dunes since that time have moved and altered their configuration so much that to-day the site even of the mansion-house is a matter of conjecture.

Traces of the orchards have been exposed at various times, however. Many years after the Barony was overthrown, the branches of a cherry-tree, in full blossom, were seen protruding from the flank of a great sand-hill, under which the gardens and orchards were believed to lie. Moreover, an old man, who died about fifty-five years ago at the age of eighty, was wont to relate that, in his youth, he had seen the branch of an apple-tree pro-

An autumn day among the wind-rippled sands, below which lies the Buried Barony. Dimly visible in the background is the Moray Firth

Marram-grass on the Culbin desert.  In the distance may be seen one of the largest sand-hills

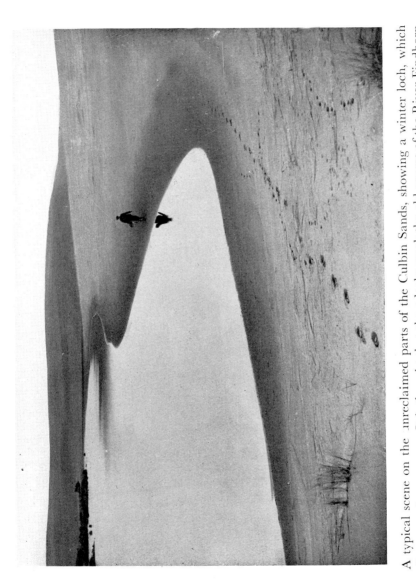

A typical scene on the unreclaimed parts of the Culbin Sands, showing a winter loch, which disappears in summer. It is thought that these lochs mark the old course of the River Findhorn

Trees planted on the Culbin about 1900 are now being engulfed by moving sand-dunes. Though between 35 and 40 feet in height, only their tops are showing.

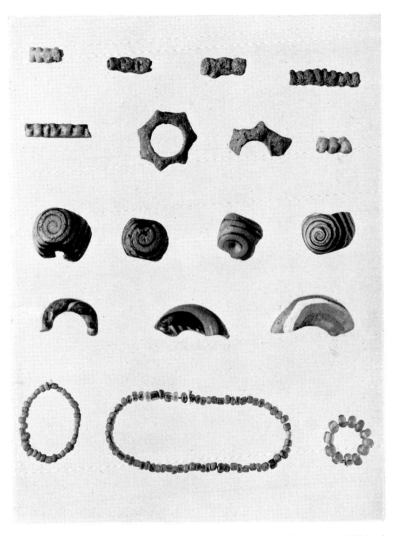

*Courtesy of the National Museum of Antiquities at Edinburgh*

Specimens of beads found at Culbin. The two upper rows are Bronze Age. The next two are Iron Age. The necklaces shown in the bottom row have been made up from beads of more recent date

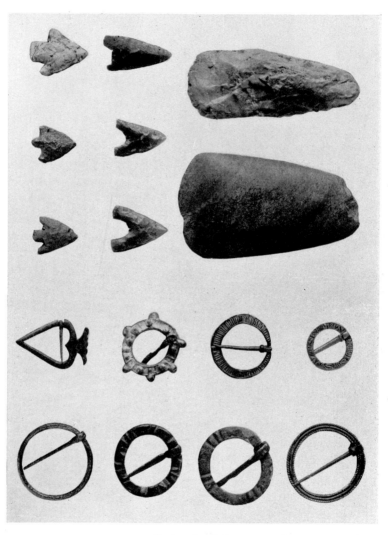

*Courtesy of the National Museum of Antiquities at Edinburgh*

Stone axes of the Neolithic Period, flint arrow-heads, and specimens of brooches of the 14th and 15th centuries and later, found at Culbin. The heart-shaped brooch is a " Huckenbooth " of the 18th century

Bent, or marram-grass, is planted to bind the sand

A threatening sand-storm among the Culbin wastes

jecting from a sand-dune. As long as the branch lay exposed to view, he inspected it from time to time. In meet season it budded and blossomed; and in the autumn it bore a quantity of apples that the old man actually gathered. They were said to have been of a fair size, and of a delicious flavour.

*   *   *   *   *

When strong winds blow upon Culbin, the sands shift with amazing rapidity, often altering the entire scene in less than an hour. Many of the mounds, measuring as much as 130 feet in height, with a base roughly 500 yards in length and over 200 yards in breadth, have disappeared completely in a night, while simultaneously sand-dunes and sand-hills elsewhere upon this desert have increased correspondingly. Scarcely ever are the sands of the Culbin at rest. The winds of the Moray Firth beat across them continually. Where the sand is not fixed with bent or with fir plantations, there is little bield of any kind in time of storm.

One of the many stories recounted in the north of Scotland, illustrating the rapidity with which a gale can alter the face of Culbin, is associated with the days when there was a considerable traffic in smuggled goods among the fishing communities of the Moray Firth. One night, when smuggling was in its heyday, a foreign vessel, laden with a cargo of contraband, arrived off the Culbin coast. As circumstances of a temporary nature precluded the owners from transferring the cargo to those for whom it was designed, it was resolved to stow it somewhere among the sand-hills until morning. The crew mustered all its resources, there-fore; and the cargo was duly concealed at the base of a sand-hill. However, during the small hours a violent gale sprang up, with the result that, when the smugglers sought their *cache* on the following morning, they could not locate even the sand-hill —so completely altered was the landscape!

News that the cargo had been lost soon spread among those who had an interest in it. Search-parties were organized, equipped with carts, spades, shovels, and with long sticks for the prob-ing of the sands. The whole of the following night was spent in feverish search. Deep trenches were even cast in the flanks of the sand-hills. But, although the moon shone brightly, rendering

9

operations as easy as could have been expected in the circumstances, all efforts to recover the lost treasure were unavailing. For some time afterwards unsuccessful attempts were made at varying intervals to retrieve this contraband, which is said to have consisted mainly of brandy and tobacco. So, to this day the smugglers' cargo lies hidden beneath the sands that have buried a barony.

According to another story, the Laird of Culbin, reputed to have been incurably addicted to card-playing, spent the eve of the tragedy in a prolonged game with one of the neighbouring tenants. Though, as time wore on, the tenant repeatedly expressed the desire to be permitted to go, that he might attend to his cattle, the Laird always managed to persuade him to stay a little longer. They were both enjoying the game; and, as the Laird put it, there seemed no immediate hurry for interrupting it merely because a gale was blowing outside. Gales were no new experience to the dwellers on Culbin. When at length the Laird went to the door to ascertain why daylight was so long in making its appearance, he discovered that his mansion had been buried overnight. Local tradition asserts that the 'neighbour' was obliged to make his exit by the chimney, and that, when so doing, the Laird, who meanwhile had lost heavily at the card-playing, found him to have been the Great Mischief—the Devil Himself! He had cloven hooves and a tail!

\*    \*    \*    \*    \*

The sand-hill, beneath which lies the Culbin Smithy, still goes by the name of the Armoury. With it are connected many strange traditions, not the least absorbing of which is that telling of the clandestine dealings Rob, the smith of the Culbin, had with Sir Robert Gordon, third baronet of Gordonstoun, better known as the Warlock Laird—he who, in order to ensure that the Devil might never take him by surprise, nor corner him, erected on his estate that group of farm buildings known, paradoxically, as the Round Square—he who, moreover, had that illuminating correspondence with Secretary Pepys about the sea-pump he had invented, and which the latter was instrumental in having introduced into the Navy. This correspondence, incidentally, is in the possession of the Warlock Laird's descendants.

It was preserved at Gordonstoun until Sir William Gordon Cumming sold that property some years ago and it was converted into a boys' school. Now it may be seen at Altyre House, near Forres, together with the crucibles, retorts, bellows, and such-like implements used by the Laird in his laboratory.

In the matter of his sea-pump, Sir Robert had the assistance of Rob, the Culbin smith, who, in point of fact, was employed by him to forge, at the Armoury, certain parts of it. Quite naturally, then, Rob's associations with a man so proficient in warlockry, in wizardry, that it was popularly believed his person cast no shade (or, as Scott put it,

> *His form no darkening shadow traced*
> *Upon the sunny wall*)

soon earned for him a reputation for black magic. As if his skill in the fashioning of 'elf-bolts'—those minute arrows of death, such as he gave to Isabel Goudie, the celebrated Auldearn witch, for her nefarious purposes—had not already won for him this distinction! No one ever probed the privacy shared by Rob of the Culbin and Sir Robert, the Warlock. But in the ancient Province of Moray everyone believed that the latter was in touch with various secret and sinister societies, such as that at Padua, and that only those most highly skilled in diablerie enjoyed with him the distinction of being able to dispense with their shadow.

★　　★　　★　　★　　★

More than a century elapsed after the final overthrow of Culbin before any attempt was made at reclamation. But from 1839, when Grant of Kincorth started planting on the eastward side of the area, in order to arrest the movements of a number of menacing sand-hills, until the present day, several successful efforts have been made. To some considerable extent stretches of sand have been fixed by broom, by bent or marram grass, and by other plants usually found under such conditions. The stout root-stock of bent, sending its ramifications through the sand, together with its long, coarse blades, have done much to bind sand-dunes that otherwise would have shifted. The value of bent for this purpose has been recognized for centuries; and anyone familiar with the machars of the Hebrides realizes how substantially its presence has preserved low-lying pasturages from being overblown with sand.

Although innumerable sand-hills and sand-dunes at Culbin still remain unreclaimed, and are utterly devoid of vegetation of any sort, here and there throughout this desert may be found tussocks of bent implanted for the fixation of the sand. For centuries bent has been utilized for this purpose along the southern coast of the Moray Firth. And it is of more than passing interest that, as recently as 1928, a number of persons petitioned the Town Council of Burghead, in Moray, for permission to pull bent with a view to replanting it where sand threatened to engulf agricultural land.

The success attending the efforts of Grant of Kincorth soon encouraged other proprietors to begin planting, though of necessity their activities were confined to the merest fraction of the territory overblown. In course of time a fair stretch of the flatter area of the Culbin was fixed by the planting of trees. This stretch became known as Low Wood. About 1918 the late Mr. Chadwick of Binsness created on the east of Culbin a number of Corsican pine plantations. The estate of Binsness lies between Culbin and Findhorn Bay. It is certain that, had Low Wood not been replanted after the extensive timber fellings toward the close of the First World War, subsequent sand-blows would have devastated the lands already reclaimed in the vicinity by private owners.

In 1921 the Forestry Commission began to acquire land at Culbin, where it now owns approximately 5,500 acres, consisting of sand-dunes partially fixed, of many of the moving sand-hills, and of the felled and replanted woodland known as Low Wood. The Commission started planting in 1922; and, up to the time of writing, about 4,500 acres have been planted—roughly five square miles. The first plantations were confined chiefly to the areas of felled woodland, where the sand, already fairly well fixed, was covered with large quantities of heath and heather. Here the tree used mostly was the native Scots pine. In the main, these plantations are in a flourishing condition.

Dotted about this desert are several small 'winter' lochs, so-called because they are dry during the greater part of the year, and are filled with brackish water after heavy rains in time of winter and spring. The draining of these loch sites presented difficulties of a peculiar nature. Here a species of Western American pine known as the Lodgepole pine has been used. This pine was given its name by the Red Indians, since they found its straightness an advantage in the supporting of their wigwams. Many of the Lodgepoles planted in 1922, where the sand already was covered with heather, are now thirty feet or more in height.

In addition to the 'winter' lochs, this region embraces one fairly large sheet of water all the year round. It is known as the Buckie Loch, and is situated on the flatter stretch of sand lying between the sand-hills and the shallow-shelving shore of the Moray Firth. Buckie Loch, together with the marshy ground adjacent to it, obviously formed part of the Findhorn's old course. The extent to which the planting of trees has tended to dry up the whole area has been very noticeable. Not only have several of the 'winter' lochs disappeared entirely, but the Buckie Loch has contracted considerably. During a hot and rainless summer, the space it occupies is quite small in comparison with that devoted to it on many fairly recent maps.

The afforestation of dunes and of hills composed entirely of moving sand is no mean undertaking. There is no point in planting trees where the sand is in active movement, and where even a wind of short duration may alter the entire configuration of the land, since such trees are either overblown with sand, or have their roots exposed. A violent gale in such conditions readily uproots young trees, or carries away the ground in which they are planted. The fixing of the sand, therefore, is the first necessity. As a rule this is achieved by the planting of bent. Tufts of bent, consisting of leaves and of part of the root-stock, are pulled up; and these are then dibbled into the sand at a spacing of twelve inches or less. As the root-stock grows and ramifies, it binds the sand, while the leaves or blades tend to shelter the sand from the winds.

Where the wind has scooped out large, circular holes or pockets in the sand, difficulty is experienced in fixing it with bent. Such pockets, therefore, are thatched with branches of birch or broom. A certain amount of broom grows naturally on parts of the Culbin Sands; while birch is to be found upon the sites of the old lochs which are now dry, and which lie mostly among the pine plantations.

Once the sand has been fixed satisfactorily, small trees, which are two or three years old and have been transplanted once or twice in the nursery, are planted out in the sand at intervals of four to five feet. The Corsican pine is the tree that has been found the most suitable where sand tends to remain unfixed. This is due to its deep-rooting nature, enabling it to penetrate into the dry sands to find sustenance below.

The task of reclamation, begun on the areas where the sand was more fixed, is now being extended eastward to the region where lie the sand-hills which, on account of their size, present the greatest problem, and which will demand every ounce of patience, energy, and resourcefulness if they, too, are to be reclaimed from the desert. And not only do several hundred acres remain untouched as yet, but eternal vigilance is necessary on the part of the Forestry authorities to conserve such areas as have been regained. Once the sand breaks loose, it advances rapidly, and may threaten to encompass a flourishing plantation. Corsican pines planted by a private owner on the Binsness estate about 1900 are now in process of being buried in moving sand. In some cases, where these trees have attained a height of thirty-five feet, no more than a foot or two now protrude above the sand-drifts. Thus it is important that, where planting and thatching operations are in progress, the sand should not be disturbed unnecessarily—which explains why the Forestry Commission has felt obliged to limit the public's access to the Culbin Sands.

With the planting of trees, parts of Culbin became infested with rabbits. Soon much of the land reclaimed was turned into a veritable warren, to the detriment of the young, struggling plantations. Writing of Culbin in 1878, a chronicler makes the following reference to the rabbits' activities:

"The rabbits ought to be well clothed, as they nibble the furze into regular cushions and ottomans, on which they sit and look out in the fine summer evenings, without fear or dread of the sharpness of the thorns, which in this arid district appear to be more penetrating than elsewhere. . . . Whatever the rabbits and hares feed on, they are larger there than in the more cultivated and fertile parts of the country, and the foxes are like wolves in size and strength. Owing to the solitude and quietness of the place, I have seen the foxes at all hours of the day, prowling about or basking in the sun, or coolly seated on the top of the sand hills, watching my movements".

Culbin, according to this authority, abounded at that time in rabbits, hares, mallard, teal, wild swans, wild geese, and herds of roe deer. To-day there are no foxes about Culbin; and only very occasionally does a roe deer find its way into this eerie, sterile waste.

★   ★   ★   ★   ★

I write of Culbin as one having some personal knowledge of it. I have visited it on several occasions when residing in the neighbourhood of Forres. The easiest approach to this Buried Barony is by sea from Findhorn, that picturesque fishing-village of narrow, winding streets and thatched cottages, situated on the opposite side of Findhorn Bay, near the constricted entrance to the same. Findhorn was the thriving port of Forres before the sands came and silted up its bay and harbour.

★   ★   ★   ★   ★

That Culbin was a settled community from quite early times is indicated by archaeological discoveries made at varying intervals. Fragments of pottery, flint implements, pieces of iron and brass, ornaments of bronze, the stone-whorls of the old-fashioned distaff, and coins dating as far back as Roman times have been found among these sandy wastes. On more than one occasion I, myself, have picked up a number of flint arrowheads and celts where the sand, in being blown away, had exposed shingly patches of old sea beaches, or perhaps a tract of what obviously once formed part of the fertile farmlands. Tracts once cultivated and showing regular furrows are often blown clear of sand; but these are never visible for long.

In the National Museum of Antiquities of Scotland, at Edinburgh, are exhibited hundreds of fine specimens of flint arrowheads found upon such tracts at Culbin, together with some brooches of the Bronze and other Ages, jet beads, ancient fish-hooks, and ancient pins. In dealing with the antiquities of this area, it is well to bear in mind that, up till comparatively recently, it has been occupied continuously from Neolithic times, if not earlier. Perhaps the most interesting class of relics found here is the beads, since these embrace specimens of the Bronze Age, of the Iron Age (Romano-British times), and of a period comparatively modern.

15

In good weather, when there is a fair breeze blowing, and rain looks as though it were far away, antiquarians from Forres and the neighbourhood set out for the Culbin Sands in the hope of finding relics dis-covered by the wind. In several of the houses in Forres itself there are many and diverse relics that at one time or another have been picked up on this desert. Some persons, I believe, actually possess silver spoons found among the sands. Maybe, these spoons once formed part of the plate belonging to the vanished Kinnairds! On the whole, however, the relics found on the old, fertile lands belong to a period too recent to be of much interest to the professional antiquarian.

My most recent visit to the Culbin Sands was made one mild, autumn day a few years ago, when, at the outset of my day's wanderings, the sun poured down so unrelentingly upon them as to make the heat quite oppressive. Naught but the brief, spasmodic, and almost inaudible, whisperings of loose sand everywhere around me proved the existence of any air movement at all; and the delicacy of the designs left upon the face of this desert by erratic winds and their eddyings was such as one might have expected from the pen of a magician artist. The loneliness was without even the whirr of insect to relieve it. Here, in truth, was solitude absolute.

If these whisperings revived in me the hope that perhaps, after all, the world had not gone completely dead, utterly mute, it was but a matter of seconds before I realized it to be nothing more than the singing of surface sand, fleeing before wind so faint that I could not even feel it, or slithering down the leeward flank of some sand-hill too steep to be able to retain it against the precipitating influence of a whiff so gentle that only the most sensitive ventometer could have detected it.

I shall always remember the panic that on this occasion took hold of me when, at nightfall, I lost my way by the edge of one of its 'winter' lochs, deep in the heart of a Corsican pine plantation. When the wind suddenly rose, and the sand started to beat overhead in clouds, I thought my last moment had arrived. I was seized with something of the dread of being buried alive that frequently visited one as great shells burst on the plains of Flanders. Had I been stranded in the heart of the Sahara itself, I could not have felt more effectively cut off from the rest of the

*Above :* Ploughed sand " carse " preparatory to planting

*Below :* Erosion of old trees at Findhorn Hill Wood

Old ploughed fields at Culbin, from which the winds have blown away the sand

*Above :* Thatching the sand with broom and branches of birch,
preparatory to planting with young trees

*Below :* The gradual reclamation of a loch site by the planting of
various species of fir

world. Even when I succeeded in emerging, fear that I might perish was still with me. I found myself alone, and in the midst of unutterable desolation and sterility. I could hear nothing but the hissing of the driven sand—see nothing but sand-hills and sand-dunes moving ominously around me—feel nothing but the sting of sand-storm upon my face and hands. I was now able to picture, from first-hand experience, the catastrophe that over-threw the Barony of Culbin in the autumn of 1694, and ruined the hapless Kinnairds.

When, at length, I managed to penetrate as far inland as Kin-corth, I paused to utter a sigh of great relief for my deliverance. By this time every pocket of my clothing was full of sand, and my watch had stopped. An hour or two later, when removing a spool from my camera by the fireside of a friend in Forres, I discovered that both the inside of the lens and the inner walls of the bellows were covered with a thin film of very fine sand. Some time afterwards, I handed my watch to a watchmaker in Glasgow, who took great pride in his workmanship. When I called for it a few days later, he rebuked me for my having subjected it to what he considered had been outrageous treatment. He had spent much time, he said, in removing sand from its works, which tempted me to proffer the suggestion that it might be considerably advantageous to his bank-balance, if he could induce his watch-owning clientèle to spend a day at Culbin when the sands were on the move!

My experience recalled Lachlan Shaw's powerful description of a Culbin sand-storm, in which he himself had been caught:

"Moving onward with eyes shut . . . I was met by a blast of wind which seemed to be a work altogether beyond the common operations of nature. The quantity of sand must have been immense. I caught it by the handful as it passed. I felt as if a dozen thongs were lashing me round the body. . . . I felt a pressure of weight on my body, which had the effect of dragging me down and retarding progress, as if the power of gravitation had been increased tenfold. For a moment I stood like one petrified—perspiration starting from every pore—I put my hand into my pocket in search of a handkerchief, and found the pocket crammed with sand. I tried another: it was equally filled! Every pocket about me was filled with sand, my clothes completely saturated with it, my shoes like to burst, my eyes, ears, nostrils, and mouth were like partakers. In short, I felt myself to be nearly altogether a man of sand".[1]

[1] *History of the Province of Moray.*

The Forestry Commission is obliged not only to carry through its schemes for the afforestation of Culbin, but also to create small-holdings for forestry workers. Already nine such holdings have been established on the more fertile lands to the south. If the Commission's efforts continue to be crowned with the measure of success they already have achieved, this desert one day may rejoice and blossom as the rose, and the Buried Barony once more yield its increase.

Somewhere or other—I cannot at the moment remember where—I once read this very lovely poem on the Culbin Sands by Andrew Young:

> Here lay a fair, fat land;
>   But now its townships, kirks, graveyards,
> Beneath bald hills of sand,
>   Lie buried deep as Babylonian shards.
>
> But gales may blow again;
>   And, like a sand-glass turned about,
> The hills in a dry rain
>   Will flow away, and the old land look out;
>
> And where now hedgehog delves,
>   And conies hollow their long caves,
> Houses will build themselves,
>   And tombstones re-write names on dead men's graves.

In the meanwhile, as J. A. Steers observed in the excellent paper he read to the Royal Geographical Society in 1937, the physiographer cannot but regret that the nearest approach to a desert in the British Isles is fast disappearing. And who would venture to say that this desert may not yet prove a lucrative concern, and pay a dividend? Nowadays, it is risky to prophesy even on a matter of deserts!

# CHAPTER TWO

## SPANISH GOLD

ONE day, when wandering through the Robert Louis Stevenson Museum at 8, Howard Place, Edinburgh, where, in 1850, Stevenson first saw the light of day, my eyes rested on a piece of oak that once formed part of the Spanish galleon lying deep down among sand and silt at the bottom of Tobermory Bay, in the Isle of Mull. This fragment of a sunken galleon instantly recalled *The Merry Men*, Stevenson's fascinating tale of the storm-kelpies haunting that romantic tideway, the Sound of Mull.

Apart from R. L. S., however, few exhibits could conjure up in the mind of the Scot a more vivid concatenation of recollection. There lies enshrined in that fragment of oak the story of Spain's ascendancy and of her decline and fall, the story of a great tempest and of consequent shipwreck, the explanation for the Spanish blood said to circulate in the veins of so many of the Western Highlanders, the story of the reckless wiles of a Highland chief, and the history of much endeavour, during the last three centuries, to retrieve from the sea's floor what is believed in many quarters of the earth to be wealth untold.

On the 20th day of May, 1588, there stood out from Lisbon the Spanish Armada, a glorious array of more than a hundred war vessels, intent upon subduing Elizabeth and her queendom, for Elizabeth, among other things, had declined in marriage the hand of the Spanish King. The dreadnoughts of this fleet were the galleons; and included in the first squadron, commanded by the Duke of Medina Sidonia, was the galleon, *Florida*, or *Florencia*, a vessel of nearly a thousand tons, exceeded in size—and then merely to the extent of a few tons—only by the *Juan*, and by the flag-ship, *San Martin*.

It may be mentioned parenthetically that, while almost every account of the fate that befell the Armada refers to this particular vessel as the *Florida* (or as some variant of this name, such as *Florencia*, *Florence*, and *Galeon del Duque de Florencia*) thus identifying her as the galleon equipped by Tuscany and contributed to the Armada by the Duke of Florence, authorities on matters relating to Spain and the Armada assure us that this vessel definitely reached Spain after the storms had devastated King Philip's proud fleet, and that the vessel of our story must have been some other unit of his fleet—possibly the *San Juan Bautista*. But Richard Hales, in his *Story of the Great Armada*, appears to favour the view that it was the much smaller vessel, *San Juan de Sicilia*. Be this as it may, for practical purposes we shall continue throughout this narrative to refer to the galleon in question as the *Florida*.

Not until July, 29th, 1588, and after divers mishaps and vicissitudes, were the pompous sails of Spain's war galleons sighted off the Lizard, and Drake, Frobisher, Howard, Hawkins, Seymour, and others given an opportunity of joining issue with them. The long-expected invasion of the English Channel had come at last. So, too, had the storm that harassed the main contingent of this tremendous fleet, with results so devastating and humiliating that for no fewer than eighty-eight of the invaders' vessels there was little means of escape except by allowing themselves to be driven through the Straits of Dover into the North Sea. Not until August, 2nd, when the surviving units of the Armada were beating a hundred miles to the east of the Firth of Forth, did the English fleet abandon the chase. About this time the Spanish admirals, conferring aboard the flag-ship, agreed that any hope of reaching Spain by the English Channel had to be abandoned. They therefore resolved to attempt a return to home waters by sailing round by the Pentland Firth into the Atlantic again. And now it was left to the winds and waves and the rock-bound coasts of Scotland and Ireland to complete what Howard and Drake and their associates had begun.

Owing to the continuance of tempestuous weather, as also to the fact that the Spanish seamen now found themselves in waters strange and unknown to them, many units of the fleet became isolated. Off the northern coast of Ireland (though some maintain it to have been the coast of Ardnamurchan, which, from a geographical point of view, is much the more probable) the *Florida*, believed to have aboard the pay-chest of the Spanish fleet, ran into foul weather at the beginning of September, and was driven from her course. By mid-September she hove-to off

Islay, southernmost of the Inner Hebrides. A week or so later, she was lying in Tobermory Bay, one of the fine, natural harbours of the Island of Mull.

\* \* \* \* \*

Perhaps the earliest reference we have to this galleon is that contained in a letter written to Walsingham, in London, presumably by William Ashley, England's Ambassador to Scotland. This letter is to be found among the Cotton MSS., and is dated Edinburgh, September, 23rd, 1588. It refers to the *Florida* as one of the largest vessels that ever sailed from Spain, commanded by a grandee of the highest order, and as having been " beaten with shote and wether ". Six weeks later its author again communicated with London concerning this straying unit of the Armada. "This 6 weeks", he wrote, "on the [west] of Scotland, a great ship of Spaigne about the Ile of Mula in MacLane's countrie, which thei here reporte cannot go from thence; those irishe people releeve them with victell, but are not able to possess her, for she is well furnished both with shott and men; if there be anie shipes of warr in Ireland, thei might have a great praie of this ship, for she is thought to be verie riche".

At a later date it was estimated that the galleon carried fifty-six guns, a large quantity of church plate, and at least thirty millions in money!

Scarcely was Walsingham in receipt of this second letter when spies in the employ of the King of Spain brought to the knowledge of the Spanish Ambassador at Paris information that a galleon belonging to the Armada had encountered dire misfortune in West Highland waters, and that the Spanish seamen manning her had lost their lives by treachery. Almost contemporaneously with this, there arrived in London a further letter from Ashley, in which he refers to the Spanish ship already mentioned by him in a previous communication. This ship, he writes, was driven by tempest to the Isle of Mull, MacLean's Country, and was destroyed there by fire, " as it is here reported by treachery of the Irishe; and almost all the men within is consumed with fire; it is thought to be one of the principalle shippes, and one of great accompt within; for he was alwais, as thei saie, served in sylver ".

Yet another illuminating account of the fate of the *Florida* is contained in a letter written at Edinburgh on November, 18th, 1588, by a certain Roger Aston to his brother :

" This daye word is come thatt the grett ship that lay in the West Iles is blown in, the eir be device of Jhon Smallett, most part of men are slein. The mauner is this Maclen enterteining greet friendship with them desirett the borrowing ii caunones and a hundredth hagbotteres to beseyge a house of Anggees Macanhales and delivered a fostores son of his as a pleg for the safe delivery of them againe in this mean tyme. Jhon Smallett a man thatt has grett trust among the Spagniardes entered the ship and cast in the powder roome a pese of lyntt and so departed within a shortt tyme after the lyntt toke fire and burnt shippe and men, whether this be true or not I am not sure, but soe his Majestie is informed ".

It is thought that John Smallett may have been one of Ashley's agents on behalf of the English Government. In any case, he informed Walsingham that the proud galleon, with all her treasure, was now at the bottom of the sea. It would appear, however, as though Walsingham kept this information to himself for some little time, since the following month (December) the Lord Deputy of Ireland was instructed to despatch ships to Tobermory for the purpose of destroying the galleon. Indeed, a month elapsed after the vessel was blown up, ere the Government was in receipt of intelligence from Ireland to the effect that a French prisoner aboard her had encompassed her doom. The news now took its course in the direction of Madrid, where contemporary Spanish documents soon confirmed the loss of this galleon in a West Highland harbour.

According to the *Irish State Papers*, it was not until the 11th of February of the ensuing year that the official account of the incident was brought to the notice of the Privy Council. We learn from this account that, of those aboard, only two or three survived, they having been blown on to the shore with the galleon's upper deck, " so that nothing was saved that was in her at that instant, and what remained unburned is now sunke under water ".

Some measure of confirmation of all this is given by David Moysie in his *Memoirs of the Affairs of Scotland*, 1577-1603. " In the beginning of October (1588), one of the great ships was drove in at the Mull of Kintyre [? Island of Mull], in which there were five hundred men or thereby ; she carried threescore brass cannon in her, besides others, and great store of gold and silver. She was soon after suddenly blown up by powder, and two or three hundred men in her, which happened by some of their own people".

Let us now examine the circumstances culminating in the extraordinary destruction of this galleon.

It so happened that the arrival of the Spaniards in these parts synchronized with a bitter feud between Lachlan Mor MacLean of Duart and MacDonald of Islay, a feud that had thrown a large part of the Western Highlands into a state of rapine and disorder. The inhabitants of the surrounding countryside, therefore, were in fine fighting fettle when the galleon came in their midst. Her captain, Don Fareija, a nobleman of Spain, found, however, that the vessel sorely needed replenishing in the matter of food-stuffs and the like. Both her tankards and larders were seriously depleted. In order to rectify these deficiencies, he made certain haughty and threatening demands upon the natives. But, as the *Register of the Privy Council* shows, MacLean of Duart was not slow to demonstrate that the wants of the distressed stranger should be attended to after he had been taught a lesson of more courteous behaviour. That he might have such a lesson as speedily as his wants seemed pressing, he was invited to land and supply his wants by the forcible means threatened, for it was not the custom of the Chief of the MacLeans to pay attention to the wants of a threatening beggar!

Eventually, however, MacLean and Don Fareija came to what, on the surface at any rate, appeared to be an amicable settlement. The latter was soon obliged to realize that his circumstances warranted discretion rather than valour. Thus it was that he now expressed his willingness to pay in gold for any provisions or services rendered to him by the islanders of Mull. MacLean of Duart immediately saw in this an opportunity for obtaining valuable assistance in the feud in which he then was engaged against MacDonald of Islay. So he concluded with Don Fareija an agreement that, as part of the payment, he should have the loan of a hundred of the Spaniards to assist him both in the defence of Duart Castle, and in a punitive expedition he was contemplating to the Small Isles—Rum, Eigg, Canna, Muck—the property of his adversary, MacDonald of Islay. With the co-operation of the Spanish mercenaries, MacLean successfully ravaged these islands with fire and sword, destroying the inhabitants in wholesale manner, regardless of sex or age. Flushed with the success that had attended this expedition, he now directed his attention to the lands belonging to MacDonald of Ardnamurchan, and laid siege to the ancient stronghold of Mingary, situated down by the shores of the Sound of Mull, in the shadow of Ben Hiant. The siege was abandoned, however, when it was learnt that a force despatched by the Scottish Privy Council was pushing forward to the castle's relief. Meanwhile Don Fareija was becoming increasingly uneasy. The wild and inhospitable nature of the country, the barbarous vendetta then engaging the entire attention of the greater proportion of its inhabitants, together with the adverse circumstances that had brought him thither, were scarcely conducive to the peace of mind of a Southerner of Don Fareija's calibre. To quit West Highland waters he therefore became more than impatient. This strange diversion of killing, into which lack of supplies had necessitated his being drawn, began to weigh heavily upon him. Visions of never reaching his destination loomed ominously before him—and for reasons more serious than were patent to him at the time.

Such was the Spaniard's frame of mind when he sent to MacLean a peremptory message to the effect that, as he was now on the point of sailing for Spain, his men must rejoin the ship without delay. This forced MacLean to retire from Ardnamurchan. On his return to Mull, he found that, during his absence, the MacDonalds, with the aid of English auxiliaries, had been showing to the properties of his clansfolk attentions not dissimilar to those he and his Spanish accomplices had been showing to theirs. On the whole, however, MacLean's visitations seem to have proved more extensive and more thorough, since we find that he was denounced as a rebel the following year.

Incensed as was MacLean by Don Fareija's having recalled his men at a moment so critical, he was whipped into fury when it came to his notice that the galleon was preparing to depart ere he had received the gold agreed upon. Determined not to be cheated, he allowed the Spaniards to return to their vessel, with the exception of three of her principal officers. These he detained as hostages until such time as the Spanish commander saw fit to implement his bargain in full.

Matters now assumed the aspect of stalemate. The hostages remained in Duart's hands: the promised gold in the Spanish commander's. In the hope of collecting what was due to him, Duart then sent aboard the *Florida* a kinsman of his own, Donald Glas MacLean, one of the sons of John Dubh MacLean of Morven. But the Spaniards took the view that, as long as any of their countrymen remained in Duart's hands, they were not disposed to enter into further negotiations. They detained Donald Glas in like manner, disarmed him, and promptly threw him into the galleon's lazaretto. At the peril of his life, they cautioned him against making any attempt at communicating with his kinsmen on shore. Highland chief and Spanish grandee now reached complete deadlock. Hostages were at their respective mercy. But one insignificant, though valiant, clansman, held in durance vile aboard a Spanish warship, was poor compensation for three comely Spanish officers incarcerated in Duart Castle. Could Don Fareija seriously contemplate quitting the shores of Mull, for all the provisions for which he had but rendered services of rapine and had paid no gold, leaving his proud countrymen to their fate at MacLean's hands? Could Donald Glas, on the other hand, accept his imprisonment with meekness, if there appeared the remotest chance of his being able to prevent the galleon's departure, even at the risk of sacrificing his own life? There was as much in the Highland pride of this uncouth islesman as in the disdainful attitude of the haughty Don Fareija.

Having discovered that little more than a thin partition separated the lazaretto from the galleon's powder-magazine, Donald Glas pierced a hole through this partition in the night-time, and, in a manner as inconspicuous as possible, laid a train of powder with the object of blowing up the entire ship, if Don Fareija finally decided to sail away with him as captive, and without his having paid to Duart the promised gold.

According to tradition in the Western Highlands, Donald Glas on the following morning was brought on deck by his Spanish captors, that he might take a farewell glance at the land of his fathers. Thereafter he was committed to his prison for the last time. Overhead he could hear the rattle of block and tackle, and of the capstan weighing the anchor, the flapping of canvas as it took the wind—and he still in captivity! No sooner was the

*Florida's* cable on board, her sails filling to the breeze, than he fired his carefully laid train of powder.

Thus, with three hundred souls aboard, this wandered unit of the Spanish Armada was blown up in Tobermory Bay, before the very eyes of Duart's hostages, and of Donald Glas's kinsfolk, who were assembled on the foreshore of Mull when the proud galleon stood out as if to sea. With her perished the resourceful Donald Glas, avenging his clan. It was estimated that only three Spaniards survived the explosion, and that, on the following day, one of the three succumbed to his injuries.

*   *   *   *   *

The foregoing is the story that for centuries has been handed down as to the final fate of the *Florida*. Irrespective altogether of tradition, historical records are all in agreement as to the main facts concerning her doom. "A ship of *Florence*", wrote Archbishop Spottiswoode in 1665, "driven upon the West Coast of Scotland, was spoiled and set on fire by certain Highlanders". Commenting on an entry in the *Register of the Privy Council*, that assiduous historian, Gregory, in enumerating the doings of Lachlan Mor MacLean of Duart, mentions that the *Florida* was blown up "by a plot of Maclean; for which offence he took out a remission, 20th, March, 1588-9". The remission, granted under the Privy Seal, was in respect of his having slain the inhabitants of the Small Isles. In this deed of pardon, Lachlan Mor is specifically accredited with "art and part plotting of felonious burning and blowing up by sulphurious gunpowder of a Spanish ship and of the men and provision of the same near the Island of Mull". And it is clearly stated that his having encompassed the destruction of this ship was *not* included in the remission. " . . . *except for his part in the destruction of the Spanish ship at Mull* " were the words used when the Privy Council attempted to lure MacLean to the Scottish Capital with the promise of a free pardon for his many misdemeanours. This is of interest in that it illustrates how little regard the Crown authorities had for the lives of the Highland clansmen. That Lachlan Mor had been responsible for the slaughter of any number of the King's subjects when he ravaged the Small Isles, for example, now seemed of minor account. The Crown probably looked upon all the warlike and rebellious clans as an intolerable nuisance, and cared little, therefore, if they exterminated one another in their feuds. It was quite obvious that, as long as the chiefs participated in civil strife that meant the devastating of one another's lands and effects, it was impossible for the Crown to obtain from them such rents and services as they legally were obliged to contribute. But the scuttling of a foreign vessel in waters over which the Crown had some jurisdiction, at least in theory, and the death of the foreign sailors aboard her, were quite a different kettle of fish! The differentiation, so exaggerated at this time, must have been based rather on the ground that the blowing up of the galleon deprived the authorities of ready access to a great store of Spanish gold than to its having robbed a few hundred seamen of their lives.

After the sinking of the *Florida*, the Spanish hostages held by Duart were liberated. They found their way to Edinburgh, where they complained to King James against Duart, both in respect of his unlawful detention of them, and of the loss of their ship. The King received their complaint with sympathy and courtesy; and arrangements were made for their immediate return to Spain. Some time later, MacLean of Duart and MacDonald of Islay appeared before the Privy Council to answer an endless list of charges, among which was the indictment that, in their internecine struggles, they had employed foreign troops. The former had used Spanish sailors : the latter had hired English mercenaries. Each chief was amerced to the extent of twenty thousand pounds Scots.

\*    \*    \*    \*    \*

From the day that the *Florida* went to the bottom of Tobermory Bay until the present time, she has attracted those interested in treasure-trove. The quantity and value of the treasure said to have gone down with her is very debatable. But, if it be true that she was one of the Armada's pay-ships, the gold she carried may have been considerable. According to one estimate, she sank with thirty million ducats, and a quantity of valuable plate. Taking the ducat as having been worth approximately ten shillings at that time, this would mean that the gold aboard her was valued at roughly £15,000,000. This figure, clearly, is fantastic. More recent and more balanced estimates have put the value of the sunken treasure at about £1,000,000.

In February, 1641, just fifty-three years after the galleon was lost, the Earl of Argyll obtained from Charles I. a gift of her, on condition that he paid to the Duke of Richmond and Lennox, then Lord High Admiral of Scotland, the one-hundredth part of the vessel, after he had deducted any expenses incurred in salving her. Since that time, the wrecked galleon has remained in the possession of the Argyll family; and accounts of the agreements entered into in connection with it between different represent-atives of that family and prospective treasure-seekers, dating from 1641 up to modern times, forms one of the most fascinating chapters in the history of British treasure-trove.[1]

In 1661 an expert Swedish diver was employed by Archibald Campbell, ninth Earl of Argyll (he who was executed in 1685) to locate and report on the condition of the wreck. The diver reported that, during the low spring tides, the galleon was lying in eight fathom at the bow, and in eleven at the stern, that the deck and a large part of the sides fore of the mizzen had been blown off by the explosion, that considerable quantities of sand and mud had accumulated in the hold, and that the poop, which was not seriously damaged, was standing up. It is more than likely that, during the first decade or two after she was sunk, the MacLeans may have made somewhat crude attempts to recover treasure from her, since she then lay in about fifty feet of water. On calm, bright days her top deck must have been visible in the clear water of Tobermory Bay. What success may have attended the efforts of the treasure-seeking clansmen, we do not know. All we can assume is that it was meagre. To-day it is esti-mated that, since the explosion, the galleon has sunk in the sand and mud to a depth of between thirty-five and forty feet.

The same Earl of Argyll again employed divers in 1665. The chief expert among them was James Mauld, who is said to have been a Swede, and who may have been the diver engaged on the wreck in 1661. Mauld, who along with his assistants had been guaranteed board and lodgings for three years, together with adequate personal protection while employed in these wild parts,

[1] The more important of these agreements may be referred to in the Appendix to the Sixth Report of the Royal Commission on Historical Manuscripts.

descended with a huge diving-bell to explore the galleon. The wreck he located without difficulty; and the chart he prepared of its position has been utilised many times by subsequent adventurers who have sought to recover something of the treasure believed to lie with the *Florida*. Mauld succeeded in bringing up some Spanish guns. After some months' diligent search, however, he abandoned the project.

Another attempt was made during the lifetime of the ninth Earl of Argyll, when a contract was entered into between him and John St. Clair, minister of Ormiston, in East Lothian, who in turn sub-contracted the undertaking with Hans Albricht von Treibelon. Somewhere about 1677 a record of several operations was made. In this the galleon is referred to as the *Admiral*, of Florence. She is described as a vessel carrying fifty-six guns, and money to the tune of thirty million—probably thirty million ducats! It was about this time that Charles II. disputed the legality of Argyll's claim; and in the lengthy litigation that ensued the Crown was defeated, and the sole right of Argyll established.

The next we hear about the sunken galleon is from Sir William Sacheverell, Governor of the Isle of Man, who inspected the diving operations going on in 1672. "Italy itself", wrote Sacheverell, "with all the assistance of Art, can hardly afford anything more beautiful and diverting; especially when the weather was clear and serene, to see the Divers sinking three-score foot under water, and stay sometimes above an hour, and at last returning with the spoils of the Ocean; whether it were Plate, or Mondy, it convinced us of the Riches and Splendour of the once thought Invincible Armada".

A spell of bad weather seems to have visited Mull about this time; and Sacheverell, who appears to have had a financial interest in the attempt to salve this Spanish treasure, gave it up in disgust, and employed his time more profitably in touring Mull and the adjacent Isle of Iona.

★　　★　　★　　★　　★

Our next important reference "anent ye Ship sunck in Tippermorie in ye Sound of Mull" is dated 1683, and is to be found in a document in the Bodleian, based upon information furnished by a professional diver named Archibald Miller. "The Ship's name is the *Florence* of Spaine. The Ship lyes sunck off the Shoare about one finger stone cast, her Sterne lyes into the Shoare Norwest, and her head to the Southeast, shee lyes under ye water at ye deepest nine fathom at Low water, and twelve fathom at full Sea or High water". This document proceeds to give details of the wreck. From it we learn that it was strewn with a great quantity of timber, and that, with the exception of the poop, it was without a deck. Amidships, Miller found three guns lying among a supply of shot. Ballast stones and shot lay on the fo'c'sle. In the stern he noticed a number of whitish-blue dishes, which might have been plate. He located, and assisted in raising, a great gun measuring eleven and a half feet in length, with a bore of seven and a half inches, and also a silver bell weighing about four pounds. Lying some little way from the galleon, he found several smaller guns, slings, falcons, and anchors. According to this expert diver, "the properest time to Dive is to begin about ye twentieth of May, and continue untill ye midst of August".

Miller, who is referred to in a contemporary document as a "dowcar in Grinok" (diver in Greenock) worked earnestly at the wreck for several weeks, during which time he made a great number of descents. On one occasion he "found a Crowne or Diadem, and had hooked the same, but being chained, it fell among ye Timbers. This Crowne is also in ye Spanish Records. I thinck ye Goods of ye Ship", he continues, "may be recovered provided ye Timber could be taken away". Through lack of financial backing and adequate diving apparatus, Miller eventually was obliged to abandon his quest.

Yet another endeavour to redeem Spanish treasure was made in 1687, when the Duke of Argyll engaged the services of a certain William Phipps, who had invented more up-to-date diving equipment. With what results Phipps laboured, one does not know, since there appears to be extant no record of his efforts.

An interesting reference to the salvage attempts made during the latter half of the seventeenth century is that provided by Martin Martin, writing about 1695:

"One of the Ships of the Spanish Armada, called the *Florida*, perished in this Bay, having been blown up by one Smallet of Dunbarton, in the year 1588. There was a great Sum of Gold and Mony on board the Ship, which disposed the Earl of Argyle, and some Englishmen, to attempt the Recovery of it; but how far the latter succeeded in this Enterprise is not generally well known; only that some pieces of Gold and Mony, and a Golden Chain, was taken out of her. I have seen some fine brass Cannon, some Pieces of Eight, Teeth, Beads, and Pins, that had been taken out of that Ship. Several of the Inhabitants of Mull told me that they had conversed with their Relations that were living at the Harbour when this Ship was blown up; and they gave an account of the admirable Providence that appear'd in the Preservation of one Doctor Beaton (the famous Physician of Mull) who was on board the Ship when she blew up, and was then sitting on the upper Deck, which was blown up entire and thrown a good way off; yet the Doctor was saved; and liv'd several Years after".

★ ★ ★ ★ ★

During the next half-century or so, attempts to salve the *Florida,* either directly by members of the Argyll family, or indirectly by adventurers and speculators authorized by them to do so, were erratic. Earlier operations had been handicapped seriously by the bellicose attitude of the MacLeans. Though Lachlan Mor was well dead and buried, his successors at Duart never quite forgot that the Spaniards owed them at least some of the wealth said to lie in the wreck. For generations the MacLeans challenged the right of the Argylls to the wreck; and a certain Eachunn MacLean, determined that divers imported from abroad would not wrest from the ocean, either for themselves or for Argyll, such treasure as the galleon may have contained, erected a small fort at a spot overlooking the scene of operations. Eachunn (Hector) and his henchmen frequently drove the divers away from the scene. To this day one may see by the shore of Tobermory Bay the ruins of the fort, from which he harried those claiming the right to search for Spanish gold.

Probably the most important attempt to salve this treasure was that instituted by the second Duke of Argyll in 1740, when a huge diving-bell, capable of being lowered about seventy feet, was used. Doubtless, the bit of wood from the galleon, which Sir Walter Scott presented to George IV. on the occasion of his visit to Edinburgh, was recovered during this attempt, as also the piece of the wreck with which Thomas Pennant was presented by an old inhabitant of Mull, "to be preserved in memory of this signal providence, so beautifully acknowledged by Queen Elizabeth, in the motto of the medal struck on the occasion: '*Afflavit et dissipantur* '".

In 1740 a considerable number of gold and silver coins was retrieved, and also a fine bronze cannon measuring nearly eleven feet in length. This cannon was wrought at Fontainebleau by the Florentine, Benvenuto Cellini, for Francis I. of France, whose arms it carries. It also bears Cellini's monogram, and a fleur-de-lys design. To-day it is to be found in front of Inveraray Castle, seat of the Duke of Argyll. It is believed to have been captured by the Spaniards during some contest—probably at the Battle of Pavia. This cannon was fired in 1854, during the celebrations following the news of Alma.

\* \* \* \* \*

After the diving operations of 1740, no further attempt appears to have been made until 1870. About that time, the late Duke of Argyll, then Marquis of Lorne, who always exhibited a marked interest in matters antiquarian and had studied carefully the old charts and documents at Inveraray Castle relating to the wreck, engaged the services of a Clyde diver called Gush. On this occasion, to use the Marquis's own words, "a few pesetas, a piece of worm-eaten oak, and a brass stanchion" were brought up. Thereafter the wreck was left unexplored until the beginning of the present century.

In 1903, more than three centuries after the lawless MacLeans had sent the vessel to the bottom, a small syndicate of Glasgow underwriters was formed for the purpose of ascertaining whether the great improvement that had taken place in diving apparatus might not enable more modern divers to salve what their predecessors had failed even to discover. With the Duke's permission, and under the direction of a certain Captain Burns, a fresh expedition arrived at Tobermory with the most recent type of dredger, with powerful submarine lamps, etc. The diver was James Gush, son of the diver employed by the Marquis in 1870. The syndicate bore the entire expenses of the search; and it was so encouraged by the discovery, during the first season, of a collection of encrusted swords, arabesques, stone balls, and doubloons bearing the names of Ferdinand and Isabella and Don Carlos, that in 1905 it entered into a five years' agreement with the Duke, and brought more elaborate and powerful equipment to the scene of its activities. Attempts were also made to photo-

*Above :* Treasure hunting in Tobermory Bay, July, 1927. The men seen in the low craft in the middle-distance are pumping air down to the diver

*Below :* One of " a number of dishes both great and small of a white blewish colour," which Archibald Miller saw from his diving-bell in 1683

*Above :* Treasure chest recovered from the *Florida*, and now at Inverawe, Argyll

*Below :* Bronze cannon bearing the monogram of Benvenuto Cellini, recovered in 1740, and now at Inveraray Castle

Inform by Archbald Miller          423

About the Ship Sunck in Typermouie in ye
Sound of Mull, The Ships name is the fflorance
of Spaine.

The Ship lyes Sunck off the Shore, about one finger throwbeast
her Sterne lyes into the Shore Norwest, and her Head to the
Southwest, shee lyes under ye Water at ye deepest Nine fathom at
a Low water, & twelve fathom at a full Sea or High water.

There is no Deck upon her Except in ye Hinder part, there
is one great heap of Timber wch I take to be the Cabbin, I did
see one doore there wch I take to be the Steerage doore, and
within that doore I did see a number of Dishes both great &
small of a White blewish Colour, but whether they are powther
or plate I know not.

Neer this place, I did see one great Gun & her Mussle in
no right an end, as big or bigger than the Gun I lifted wch would
carry 48ll ball, there is a great heap of Cannon that about
Midshie, & upon the Shet lyes three Iron Guns.

In the fore part of the Ship lyes many great Ballast stones
& some shot amongst them, & there was found one Silver bell
about 4ll weight, wee got without the Ship at a very distance
the six great Gun wth other two (all Brass Guns) the great Gun
is eleaven foot length, & seaven inches & one fourth part
of measure in ye bore, th'other two were Minions, wee also
got two Demy Culverins, two falcons, two slings all Brass.

Wee lifted three Anchors whereof one was eighteen feet
of length, th'other was fifteen and the third was ten, I got
two brass sheaues weighing sixty pound, I lifted also the
Rother, & took eight Iron pykes of it, it was twenty eight foot
of Length, but there was one peece broken of the same.
I lifted the Komo stone of Curious worke, pauled wth a
                                                       Spring

Courtesy of J. D. W. Treherne

Passymaster disk (left) and plate, recovered in 1919 and photographed from a negative

graph the floor of the bay; and for several weeks powerful pumps sucked away at a bank of sand and silt, some twenty feet in height, which was believed to have accumulated over the hull. A digger was also used on this bank. Among the thickly corroded relics found were copper powder-pans, pike-blades, shot, several small coins, and a heavy candlestick of silver. But, for all the pumping and digging, the actual position of the wreck still baffled the searchers. The idea that the bank of silt, most of which by this time had been sucked away, concealed the hull seemed improbable by 1906. During that year, over eight acres of Tobermory Bay, from a depth of six to fourteen fathom, were dredged and examined; and a well-known diviner, Stearns by name, was brought on the scene. The diviner's rod appeared to respond to the presence of precious metals—gold and silver—and this gave the syndicate renewed hopes. The services of a mining expert were also enlisted at this time. However, little treasure of any consequence was recovered; and in the following year the syndicate's contract expired.

But the quest for the *Florida* and her treasure was resumed in 1909, when a London syndicate was formed under the direction of the late Colonel K. M. Foss, an American, who secured for the enterprise a great deal of press publicity, but comparatively little treasure. Before starting operations, he had searched, with commendable diligence, the pages of history, not only in this country, but also in France and Italy, in Spain and in Portugal. When thus engaged, he became more and more convinced that Davy Jones's Locker, at the bottom of Tobermory Bay, contained wealth to the value of roughly £300,000. It is doubtful whether there exists a State document referring to the Armada which he omitted to consult. Forthwith, he applied to the Duke of Argyll for a lease of the salvage rights in the wreck. Embedded in sand and silt, at a depth of some thirty feet, eighty-four yards from the pier at Tobermory, and in forty-eight feet at low water, Colonel Foss discovered, in 1912, what he believed to be the sunken *Florida*. In his preliminary attempt at salvage, according to one newspaper account, he succeeded in penetrating a great bank of "hermit crabs, clams, cockles, and huge, hoary oysters from half an inch to four-and-a-half inches thick, the latter flattened out by the pressure of myriads which had evidently crushed the life out of one another within the wooden walls of the old galleon".

Dredging operations proceeded apace. Every tiny object that looked as though it might have belonged to the wreck was washed and sieved with meticulous care. Yet, it was some time before there came up from the sea's floor anything that could have been regarded as encouraging. Imagine Foss's delight, then, when one day the 'grab', tenaciously clinging to something that refused to allow itself to be raised to the surface, was suddenly freed, and came up, holding in its massive jaws the 56-lb. breech-block of Italian origin, which was afterwards on show at the Wembley Exhibition! Some Spanish daggers, salved at a later date, were on view at the Earl's Court Exhibition; and a large sword brought up about this time was sent to a well-known jeweller in the West End of London to have much encrustation removed. Thereafter it was placed in the window; but the crowd it attracted occasioned so much obstruction that the police had to request its removal to a position less prominent.

Colonel Foss also recovered one or two silver spoons, some doubloons and pieces-of-eight, and a number of pewter plates, all of which were carefully cleaned and examined. Many of the plates were eventually restored. In all probability, these were the 'dishes' Archibald Miller had spotted from his diving-bell, nearly two and a half centuries previously. Some of them were purchased by the late Antonio de Navarro, husband of the famous actress, Mary Anderson, and in his day a prominent member of the Society of Pewter Collectors. The photograph of one of them, to be found at page 32, was given to me by their son. This particular plate measures roughly seven inches in diameter, and is rather deeper than a modern plate, though not so deep as a soup-plate. It is quite plain, bearing no pewterer's mark, and was given away by de Navarro, along with other salvaged relics, just before his death in October, 1932. A piece of the galleon's timber went, appropriately, to John Masefield. Unfortunately, the Navarro pewter pieces, bequeathed in 1933 to the Fitzwilliam Museum by his widow and son, include nothing recovered from the galleon.

A member of a well-known Glasgow firm of chartered accountants writes me that *he* owns a pewter plate from the wreck

similar to that just described. He got it from the late Alfred
Yeates, another enthusiastic collector of pewter. Yeates's collection, auctioned at Sotheby's in 1930, included "a rosewater dish
with raised central boss, dredged up in 1912 from the sunken
galleon in Tobermory Bay", and also a plate recovered at the
same time. These were sold originally by Messrs. Browett &
Taylor at the Inns of Court Hotel, London, in December of that
year. The dimensions of the rosewater dish are given as 15⅜
inches in diameter, with 1⅝ inch in rim; and the photograph
reproduced at page 33 shows what both relics looked like before
they were restored.

Between 1912 and the outbreak of war in 1914, when operations
on the wreck were interrupted, Foss recovered treasure estimated
at well over a thousand pounds in value, though it must have
been rather difficult to assess the worth of such relics so soon after
their recovery. What I mean to convey is that their value at that
time could scarcely have been viewed in due perspective.

In 1919 he resumed his activities at the identical spot, now
readily located by means of the accurate bearings made during
his previous attempt. In 1922, under a new organization known
as the Mull Syndicate, he made a third effort, having again leased
the rights from Argyll. He now employed, among others, Miss
Margaret Naylor, a diver, who made one or two descents. Miss
Naylor had been connected with the search since 1918, and
subsequently became lessee herself. In a letter she wrote me a
year or two ago, she tells me that she believes they were working
on the right spot, for she assisted in recovering the Italian breech-
block already referred to, a couple of copper blocks, and various
other objects.

In the interim, Foss had purchased from the L.C.C. a fire-
engine, the powerful jet from which, it was hoped, would wash
away, with greater rapidity than heretofore, the silt and clay in
which relics possibly lay. The fire-engine, duly mounted on a
barge, was brought to the scene of expectations. But, at the
moment when the prospect seemed brightest, calamity befell.
The hose, now working at full pressure, was accidentally turned
on Foss, injuring him severely, both internally and externally,
thus necessitating the suspension of his activities for a season or
two. Once again, however, he returned to Tobermory and

worked feverishly, but this time with little to show for his trouble and zeal. Yet, there was some consolation for Foss, in that the Duke of Argyll, having satisfied himself that the crest on a re-covered salver was a certain Spanish nobleman's, wrote to him that he had no more doubt as to the identity of the wreck than he had of his own identity.[1]

Colonel Foss died in 1934.

When I called at Tobermory on my way to the Outer Hebrides in the summer of 1927, salvage operations were still in progress. As the mail-steamer came alongside the pier, I managed to photograph one of the divers, as his head, encased in a ponderous head-piece, appeared above the surface of the bay, about a stone's-throw away. Two sunburnt seamen assisted him into the boat, and began to unscrew the head-piece. Soon he was seated on a thoft, wiping his brow, and breathing once more the free air of heaven, the morning sun a-glint on his damp hair. I called over the water to him, to enquire whether he was finding anything resembling piastres or pesetas, anything in the nature of doubloons or moidores. He answered me in the negative, with a tired shake of his head.

\* \* \* \* \*

Treasure-seekers have by no means abandoned hope of salving the *Florida's* riches. In the autumn of 1936, there disembarked at Tobermory from the motor-vessel, *Lochearn*, an experienced engineer in the person of R. van der Boom, managing-director of Van Wienen's Diving Company and Salvage Corporation, Amsterdam. He had just designed a diving apparatus for work on wrecks such as this. Meanwhile, much interest was being shown in Holland in a proposed expedition to Tobermory.

In 1937 there appeared in *Chambers's Journal* an article of mine, a much abridged version of this chapter. Some weeks later, I received a communication from a firm of Amsterdam solicitors, acting on behalf of Messrs. Van Wienen, asking me whether I could assist in convincing the people of Holland that money invested in yet another endeavour to recover treasure from Tobermory Bay stood every chance of bringing in a reasonable return. The writer was particularly anxious to know whether,

[1] The Duke's actual words are to be found in David Masters's fascinating book, *When Ships Go Down*, published by Eyre & Spottiswoode in 1932.

in the event of his coming over to this country to see me, I could show him, or at any rate put him in the way of finding, the originals of at least the more important documents quoted in my article. I assured him that I could. Scarcely had my reply been received when I had a cablegram from this gentleman, intimating that he proposed crossing from Flushing that evening, and would telephone me in the morning. He duly did so; and by 10 a.m. he and I found ourselves in serious consultation in the lounge of his hotel. He was about my own age, and spoke English perfectly. In discussing the projected expedition, he explained that a recent article in a leading Dutch newspaper, written by an acknowledged authority on matters historical, had ridiculed the idea that there lay in Tobermory Bay any wreck worth investing a guilder in. This, it appears, had influenced, adversely, many who might have thought of joining in the speculation. He was convinced, however, that, if only he could see some of the documentary evidence I had quoted—more especially, perhaps, the testimony of the diver, Archibald Miller—and possibly return to Amsterdam with photographic reproductions of certain excerpts, he would be able to counteract any harm done by the publication of the article aforesaid. *And, of course, it was to be understood that I would be remunerated handsomely for my assistance!!*

I conducted him to the British Museum, introduced him to the appropriate authorities, explained his mission and enlisted their interest and co-operation in it, spent some days with him in tracing the necessary documents, and helped him to arrange for the photographing of pertinent passages. Then I sent him off to Oxford to see what the Bodleian Library could do for him.

Aware that permission to explore the sea's floor at Tobermory would have to be obtained from the Duke of Argyll, I advised him to allow *me* to arrange that part of the business for him, on the plea that everything depended on the method of approach, and that the Scots had to be handled with great caution in matters of this kind. Determined, however, that his flying visit to this country should leave unturned no stone he himself could turn, he suddenly telephoned me from his hotel to say that he was dashing off to Scotland by the first available train from Euston, intent on interviewing the Duke at Inveraray. I tried to dissuade him from a step so precipitate, explaining certain subtleties of conduct which he did not appear to appreciate. Anyhow, off he went.

A couple of days later, he returned to London. The northern part of his mission had been a complete failure, as I had anticipated. At Inveraray he met with a somewhat discouraging reception. He failed to see Argyll, and came back in a mood of chagrin. If Argyll declined to consider leasing the salvage rights, what would be the use of all the British Museum's valuable evidence of treasure? I still have in my possession an amusing letter the Duke wrote me a day or two afterwards, declaring that he had no intention of leasing anything to any Dutchman! "Every year I get a number of letters from France and other countries upon this subject, which, as I am always busy, I have ceased even to answer. They are a perfect nuisance".

Satisfied on the fifth day that he now had seen all the relevant documents, with the exception of Archibald Miller's, and having made arrangements for certain photographic reproductions, the Dutchman phoned me that afternoon to say that, as his task in this country was accomplished, he proposed returning by the Hook that evening. And would I go to his hotel for a concluding talk over a cup of coffee, and at the same time accept from him something tangible for all my trouble? I went, largely out of curiosity, since by this time matters seemed to be taking on that aspect of urgency one associates with schemes but impulsively conceived. To his enquiry as to what my out-of-pocket expenses were, I could make no satisfactory response. Had he asked me to assess the value of my time, of my experience, and of my specialized knowledge, I would have felt happier. Rather grudgingly, I thought, he handed me two pound notes. I took them, without comment.

For a while thereafter, we sat and talked in the lounge with frankness unsurpassed. He now told me of the major ambition of his life: *he wanted an English wife*. "She must be what you British call 'of good family'," he insisted; "and she must have at least a little money". Could I possibly assist him in finding the woman he was looking for? Not only did I tell him that I thought I could, but, when he mentioned that so serious a business would entail a less hurried sojourn in this country, I instantly offered him a few weeks' hospitality at my home in Chelsea!

That evening he left for Amsterdam, more buoyed up with all I had told him of desirable Englishwomen I had in mind for him than with all his documentary evidence of treasure in Tobermory Bay. But the Second World War intervened; and that was the last I ever heard of the Diving Dutchman's projected search for Spanish Gold, or of his emissary's quest for an English wife.

But it was by no means the last I was to hear from those interested in the matter of salvage. In helping my Dutch visitor, I was indiscreet enough to send to the *Sunday Times* and to the *Observer* a brief letter-to-the-editor, seeking information on the whereabouts of the original letter written in 1683 by Archibald Miller, since the Bodleian authorities, whilst admitting that they might have it, were unable to trace it when our Dutch hero arrived in their midst. The publication of my letter brought me within a few days a veritable tornado of correspondence from all manner of people, some of whom had already been engaged on the wreck as lessees of the Duke of Argyll, and nearly all of whom wanted to give valuable information, or render services in future enterprise—usually 'for a suitable consideration'. Others sought particulars of Van Wienen's scheme. Almost without exception, interviews were sought with me; and some correspondents even went so far as to suggest my setting out on quite considerable journeys to solicit their help. One particularly attractive offer—attractive on paper, anyhow—came from the representative of an organization styling itself the Lusitania Salvage Corporation. The writer requested that I should seek to interest Van der Boom in a company he himself had registered under the imposing title of the Anglo-French Ship Recovery Company. All correspondents claimed to be in possession of more important information regarding the sunken galleon than anyone else in the world, and insisted that their co-operation would be essential to the success of any further attempt to salvage treasure. Enquiries and offers from speculators, divers, naval architects, marine engineers, and potential investors rolled in so irresistibly that I could well imagine how poor Argyll has been pestered all his life by applications to search and salvage.

★　　★　　★　　★　　★

In the Western Highlands one hears many a curious tradition

concerning the galleon at Tobermory.  According to one such, a dog belonging to a member of the crew was thrown ashore on a fragment of the galleon's deck, somewhat after the manner in which, according to Martin, Dr. Beaton found *terra firma*.  The creature was picked up in a dying condition by one of the natives, who cared for it and nursed it back to health.  It is said that it constantly resorted thereafter to the spot on the shore nearest the sunken vessel, to howl disconsolately.

Tradition also has it that Mull owes its breed of nimble-hoofed ponies to the fact that, when the galleon arrived in Tobermory Bay, she had aboard a number of ponies which the Spaniards put ashore to graze, and which in this way survived when galleon and crew perished.

Then there is the tradition concerning a Spanish princess, said to have gone down with the ship.  The body of this princess was recovered later, and interred in the ancient burying-ground at Keil, in Morven, on the opposite shore of the Sound of Mull. A year or two ago I had it from the natives of Lochaline, in Morven (with whom, incidentally, I have some filial association) that, some time after the destruction of Philip's fleet, there sailed thither a Spanish vessel, in order to bear the princess's remains to her native land.  During the exhuming of her body, however, some of her finger-bones were lost; and so at times the ghost of the princess may be seen as it flits between Keil and the shore of the Sound of Mull, seeking the lost finger-bones.

According to yet another tradition, there went down with the *Florida* a statue of the Virgin, in gold, with eyes of sapphire.  This is the golden Madonna alluded to by my friend, Dorothy Welles-ley, in her poem on Tobermory:

> Deep down in the tangle
> Where the seaweeds sway,
> I stare at the treasure
> In Tobermory Bay.
>
> I looked over the gunwale—
> Moidores for me!
> Nay, more than moidores—Madonna,
> In the depth of the sea.[1]

[1] From *Poems of Ten Years*, by the Duchess of Wellington.

# CHAPTER THREE

## THE SEA-DOGS OF SCOTLAND

THE appeal a few years ago for funds to restore the monument known as Sir Andrew Wood's Tower, situated at the Fife village of Largo, served to recall the fact so little appreciated, and possibly little recognized even by Scots people, that the Scottish nation could boast her Sea-Dogs at least two generations before the Drakes and the Raleighs were heard of. Indeed, Scotland had attained her zenith as a maritime power at a time when, to all intents and purposes, the proud English fleet of Elizabethan days was non-existent. The suggestion, therefore, that this monument, which has been allowed to fall into a sorry state of dilapidation, should be placed under the care of the Ancient Monuments Commission will be acceptable to those conversant with the skill and prowess of Sir Andrew Wood and his seamen, and with their contribution to the founding and maintenance of the Scottish navy during the latter years of the fifteenth century and the first few decades of the sixteenth.

Sir Andrew appears to have been a native of Leith, though Largo is commonly believed to have been his birthplace. In any event, after a successful career as merchant, shipowner, mariner, and naval tactician, he retired to Largo, where he built a castle for himself, and spent the remainder of his days in developing and enjoying his estate, and doubtless in dreaming of the scenes of his naval encounters and victories, just as Drake, according to Sir Henry Newbolt's fine sea ballad, lay "dreamin' arl the time o' Plymouth Hoe", nearly three-quarters of a century later.

Sir Andrew Wood died at Largo in 1515. He was interred in the ancient parish church, at a spot marked by a stone let into the floor, and simply inscribed. All that now remains of his palatial castle is the Tower, aforementioned. But the natives of Largo, with some degree of self-pride and satisfaction, still point to part of the ditch along which, according to tradition current in 'The Kingdom', ran the canal specially constructed by Sir Andrew, so as to enable him, in his declining years, to sail in his barge of state between the parish church and his residence. This barge is said to have been manned by rowers selected from amongst the old pensioners who had served with him aboard the *Yellow Carvel*, the most historic of his ships, and one of the most celebrated fighting vessels of her age.

And one September day recently, while endeavouring to photograph Sir Andrew Wood's Tower, my eyes alighted on an ancient pear-tree standing in deep, autumn-tinted grass, and bright with clusters of red fruit. Tradition has it that this tree was planted by Sir Andrew himself. "That's the way the talk goes here in Fife, anyway!" remarked one of the gardeners at Largo House, as I conversed with him while adjusting the legs of my tripod.

Incidentally, it is ironical that, although the name of Sir Andrew Wood is revered by all Scotsmen informed on their country's achievements, the only piece of popular information about Largo possessed by most dwellers north of the Tweed is that it was the birthplace of Alexander Selkirk, the prototype of Daniel Defoe's 'Robinson Crusoe'.

★   ★   ★   ★   ★

On the face of things, it seems absurd to regard mediaeval Scotland as a sea-power to be reckoned with, since so little stress has been laid on the seafaring record of the Scottish nation during the troublous reigns of James III. and James IV. A national knowledge of maritime affairs, as well as the reputation of what we still speak of as 'the Scot abroad,' have not been won in modern times : on the contrary, they date back to the days of the early Stewart monarchs. This is demonstrated largely by the fact that the bulk of books, etc., printed at this time were concerned, either directly or indirectly, with the development of Scotland's trade upon the seas. In producing treatises on maritime law, contemporary presses had as much work as they could cope with. Some further indication of the importance Scotland's mercantile marine service assumed during the reign of James III. is the extraordinary increase in litigation arising out of shipping affairs. It was claimed by Lord MacMillan a few years ago that British maritime law has been founded largely on the old Sea Laws of Scotland, enacted for the most part during the early decades of the sixteenth century. Likewise, resort to the works of almost any of the old Scots *makars*, or poets, and to the records of contemporary chroniclers, indicate the position that maritime matters occupied in the affairs of the Scottish nation. For example, Gavin Douglas, son of the traitorous Bell-the-Cat, of whom we shall read later, shows clearly his familiarity with both northern and southern waters when he alludes in his *Aeneid* to the perilous bays in the vicinity of Carthage as being "mair perellus than Yairmouth sandis or Holland coist".

Of course, in estimating a nation's naval strength in mediaeval days, we must embrace merchant vessels as well as what were described as royal ships. This was recognized by James III. when he decided to build his fleet. He found it difficult to differentiate between what strictly was a ship of war and a ship of commerce. His shipbuilding, therefore, was planned in such a way as to render it possible to convert a merchant vessel into a war vessel, or *vice versa*, with the greatest expedition. It would be impracticable— nay, impossible—to make a survey of Scotland's growth as a sea power toward the close of the fifteenth century, and during the opening years of the sixteenth, without realizing how national a part was played by her merchant fleet. And it is of interest to remember that in Scotland at this period even the King's special ships of war were used in trade and commerce, either directly by himself, or by traders to whom he hired them for commercial purposes. This was especially the case during the reign of James III. For all the criticism that, rightly or wrongly, may have been levelled against James as a monarch, it cannot be gainsaid that, largely owing to his personal interest in matters maritime, the basis was laid for the commercial prosperity that Scotland enjoyed at a later date. There is no doubt that, so far as England and her commercial allies were concerned, the dynastic weaknesses finding expression in the Wars of the Roses afforded an excellent opportunity alike for Scottish seamen and Scottish traders. During that period the Scottish export trade in wool, hides, salmon, and the like increased considerably. According to Pedro de Ayala, the Spanish Ambassador, Scottish traders had displaced, almost completely, their English competitors in the lucrative trade with Flanders and the Netherlands. Even while English trade was expanding under Henry VII., their agents were bemoaning the enterprise of the Scottish adventurers, who virtually had established a monopoly in Antwerp. Contemporaneous with this was the decline of the Hanseatic League, and the corresponding increase in the importance of the Scottish herring industry. Units of Scotland's growing merchant fleet now became engaged in importing vast quantities of salt from Spain, for the curing of the herring; and shortly afterwards iron ore was added to the list of imports from that country.

\* \* \* \* \*

Whereas in England at this time responsibility for the naval defence of the realm was placed upon a small group of favoured communities like the Cinque Ports, in Scotland the function of such defence was performed by the Royal Burghs, commensurate with their resources. In respect of this responsibility, extensive trading facilities were granted to these Burghs. Thus it was that the trade of the Scottish burgesses and the development of the Scottish navy were so interdependent. The right that the Royal Burghs regarded as the most sacred was their right to engage in foreign trade. Only the burgess of a Royal Burgh was permitted to carry on trade with a foreign country without a special licence from the Crown. And it was largely in return for this monopoly of foreign trade that the Scottish Royal Burghs were required to find one-third of the National Land Tax, the remaining two-thirds having been borne equally by the Church and the 'friehaldirs' (freeholders). It is true, of course, that at a later date many of the newer burghs, which became known as Burghs of Barony, were permitted reluctantly by the Royal Burghs to share in Scotland's expanding foreign trade. But this concession was granted them on the explicit understanding that they undertook to meet their fair share of the Land Tax. Incidentally, the burden of the Land Tax, as was pointed out recently by the writer of a learned article on the Stewarts and their navy, continued to rest on the Burghs until comparatively recently, albeit the exclusive privilege of trading abroad had been lost to them some centuries earlier.

At this time, and indeed well into the eighteenth century, Scotland's maritime activities were confined almost entirely to the east coast. This obviously meant that her trade routes were upon the North Sea, which explains the development of the ports of Aberdeen, Dundee, and Leith, long before there was any serious commercial expansion on the Clyde. Occasionally, however, Scottish traders participated in the traffic then passing through the Narrow Seas, as the English Channel and the Straits of Dover were called in olden times by the seamen of Western Europe. They were the highway not only for English shipping, but also for the proud merchant vessels owned by the maritime communities of Venice, of Genoa, and of Spain and Portugal. These communities were now developing a lucrative traffic with such seaports as Bruges, Hamburg, and Lübeck. But, as fast as the Narrow Seas offered trade routes for valuable merchandise, they became infested by the pirates of all nations. Even pirates hailing from Leith frequented southern waters. The sober merchant seamen of Leith therefore felt that, if they meant to develop a legitimate and expanding trade, they would be obliged to concentrate their attention upon the trade routes afforded by the North Sea, which at this time was comparatively free from piracy, and offered excellent opportunities for peaceful commerce between Scotland and the ports of Belgium, Holland, Denmark, and the Baltic. Thus it was that the Scottish traders found it so much to their advantage to establish and maintain a strong commercial relationship with ports like Bruges, Middelburg, and Veere, which soon became the staples, or depots, of their foreign enterprises. Through Bruges they were able to trade not only directly with Flanders, but also indirectly with France.

During this period Leith retained a position of prime importance. Not until the ascendancy of Glasgow was established, in the early decades of the nineteenth century, did Leith become the second port of the country.

With Leith, perhaps more than with any other Scottish seaport, are associated the names of Scotland's Sea-Dogs. Her development as a trading centre soon produced a rich and powerful trading class. Under the direction of skippers like Peter Falconer and Gilbert Edmonston, the town flourished. The increasing prosperity of its trading fraternity soon attracted the more enterprising and adventurous members of several titled and landed families to enter commerce, or adopt the sea as a profession. Among such Leith families, who now contributed toward establishing the merchant service of Scotland, were the Logans and the Bartons. The latter family successfully conducted a war of spoliation on the high seas against the entire maritime might of Portugal! It is said that, at the close of the fifteenth century, the number of sea captains hailing from Leith was out of all proportion to its size, and that not in all Europe was there a port that could boast mariners as skilful and as daring. Even the most casual perusal of contemporary documents shows that, had it not been for Leith's contribution to seafaring, King James IV. could neither have built nor manned his navy.

\*   \*   \*   \*   \*

One of the earliest Scottish mariners to win fame for himself, and a place of prominence for his country in the maritime world, was Sir Andrew Wood, to whom we already have alluded briefly. Wood is regarded as having been one of the most illustrious of Scotland's Sea-Dogs. He is believed to have worked his way up from humble beginnings, until he became the most powerful and influential merchant in Leith. Through his performance at sea, he was the trusted friend and naval adviser of James III., during whose reign he commanded two vessels famous in Scottish history—the *Flower* and the *Yellow Carvel*—both of which were about three hundred tons. The *Flower* was Wood's own property: the *Yellow Carvel* (a name so reminiscent of the caravels in which the merchants of Spain and Portugal visited the Far East, as well as the Americas) belonged to the King; but, in accordance with the practice at the time, Wood hired her at an agreed figure per voyage, or per annum. Formerly, the *Yellow Carvel* had been commanded by that doughty Sea-Dog, John Barton, the first of a noted family of Leith mariners.

Wood sailed frequently between Leith and the Low Countries in these two vessels; and he also visited many French ports with them. Of his voyages in the *Flower* to old Dutch ports like Bergen-op-Zoom and Middelburg, we read in that fascinating ledger in which Andrew Halyburton kept the accounts of his Scottish and Netherlands clientèle. From 1493 until 1503 Halyburton held the imposing position of Lord Conservator of the Scottish Privileges in the Low Countries; and in a private capacity he acted as agent for Scottish merchants desirous of buying or selling in the markets of the Low Countries. He was

excellently situated, therefore, for obtaining first-hand information regarding the foreign activities of the merchants of Edinburgh and Leith, and of Scotland's Sea-Dogs during the closing
years of the fifteenth century. Halyburton's ledger is now
preserved in the Register House, at Edinburgh.

It was mainly through the opportunities afforded Wood of
coming into contact with French, Portuguese, Dutch, and even
English pirates, when peacefully pursuing his commercial
relationships, that he developed his skill in naval strategy. So
successfully did he emerge from his encounters with the pirates
of various nations that, in more recent times, he often is spoken
of as the Scottish Nelson of his day. His skill as a strategist soon
commended itself to James III., who, on at least two occasions,
called upon him to defend Dumbarton Castle against the fleet
of Edward IV.

When Archibald Bell-the-Cat and other Scottish nobles rose
in rebellion against James, Sir Andrew Wood stood firm for
the King, and placed both his ships and his services at his
disposal. One of Wood's vessels carried James across the Forth,
that he might join his supporters in the North; and it is well
known that the King, in his fateful flight from the field of
Sauchieburn in June, 1488, was making for the shore of the
Firth of Forth at Alloa, whither Sir Andrew had proceeded with
a couple of ships to render him aid, and to rescue him if necessary.
Local tradition says that, for some miles along the Firth in
this vicinity, several small boats were anchored close inshore,
ready to pick up the King, should defeat befall him. But for
the mysterious occurrence at Beaton's Mill, it is improbable that
Wood's seamen would have watched this seaboard in vain for
the royal fugitive. As it was, both the *Flower* and the *Yellow
Carvel*, while cruising expectantly in the upper reaches of the
Firth, succeeded in rescuing many of James's fleeing adherents.
In fact, until news of the King's fate had been confirmed,
it was believed that he lay concealed aboard the *Yellow Carvel*,
along with some of his wounded followers.

The rebellious nobles, following upon their success at Sauchieburn, assembled at Stirling, where Prince James, a lad of fifteen,
was proclaimed King James IV. With a view to obtaining the
submission of the Capital, they then rode on to Edinburgh, and

encamped on Leith Links for a couple of days, still unaware of
what exactly had happened to the defeated monarch, whose
flight from the field of battle had been witnessed a few days
previously. By this time the *Yellow Carvel* and her consort, the
*Flower*, were riding at anchor a mile or two offshore, and in
what to-day are known to seamen as Leith Roads. The nobles
now influenced the young King to order Sir Andrew to appear
before him and his Council, that they might obtain from him
information as to the fate and whereabouts of James III. But
the wily commander declined to compear until two hostages of
rank and circumstance had been put aboard the *Yellow Carvel*
as a guarantee for his personal safety. Forthwith Lords Seton
and Fleming were placed aboard his ship, and the commander himself ordered his seamen to row him in his great barge
to the shore at Leith. He disembarked at the landing-place
opposite what was known as the King's Wark. Here he was
confronted with the young King and the victorious lords. When
questioned by the former as to whether his father, James III., was
aboard any of his vessels, Wood retorted that he only wished he
could say that he was, so that he might have the privilege once
more of defending him against his traitorous son, and those who
had conspired with him. An interesting, though perhaps fantastic, account of this incident is supplied by Lindsay of Pitscottie,
who records that, when Wood appeared before the confederate
lords, the young King hastened toward him, exclaiming : "Sir,
are you my father ?"

"I ame nocht your father", came the reply; "but I wes
your fatheris trew servand, and sall be to his autorite till I
die, and enemie to them quho wes the cause of his doune
putting!"

By way of explaining how a boy of fifteen was unable to
recognize that Wood was not his father, it has been suggested
that the commander appeared in full armour, and that his face,
on this account, was concealed. However, Bell-the-Cat and the
other rebel lords associated with him could get no satisfaction
from Wood. With reluctance, therefore, they dismissed him
to his ships. Had it not been for the two hostages aboard the
*Yellow Carvel*, his fate would, perhaps, have been otherwise.
Already his seamen were getting anxious for his safety; and, had

*Courtesy of the Royal Scottish Museum*

Model of the *Yellow Carvel*

*Courtesy of the Royal Scottish Museum*

Model of the *Great Michael*

Sir Andrew Wood's Tower at Largo

there been much more delay in his return, Seton and Fleming assuredly would have swung from the yardarm!

*     *     *     *     *

As time wore on, it became obvious that James IV. and his nobles would be obliged to come to some sort of understanding with this notable Sea-Dog and his crews. Soon after the news of the previous monarch's fate had been confirmed, Sir Andrew signified his willingness to swear allegiance to the new King, although he never quite forgave him for the part he had played in the rebellion which had culminated in the murder of his father. But it was, perhaps, as well for James that Wood was now prepared to overlook this unhappy episode, since Scotland's position, both at home and abroad, was becoming increasingly insecure. At home, the King had to contend with "the heavy murmur of the people", because nothing was being done to bring his father's assailants to a reckoning: abroad, "the auld enemie" was active in promoting strife against his authority, and in aiding and abetting piracy upon the merchant vessels belonging to his burgesses.

About this time, five English vessels sailed into the Firth of Forth, and began a systematic campaign of piracy. Immediate action against them was imperative. So, Sir Andrew Wood was directed to pursue them and, if possible, engage them. It is implied by Pitscottie, however, that Wood, as yet, was hardly acceptable to the new régime. This historian informs us that, only when all other sea captains had been approached, and had declined to stand out to sea against the English pirates, was Sir Andrew's assistance sought. Be this as it may, we do know that, despite the counsel of those who urged him to follow the English with a goodly array of vessels, he sailed down the Firth with only the *Yellow Carvel* and the *Flower*. Off Dunbar his ships came up with those of the English pirates. Undaunted by the apparent unevenness of the contest, this tried strategist blew his whistle for action. In the naval battle that ensued, the English ships were captured; and Wood in triumph escorted them into the port of Leith, where their captains and crews were held captive.

This humiliating defeat moved Henry VII. to wrath—so much so, in sooth, that he offered an annual pension of a thousand pounds to the person who succeeded in defeating or in scuttling

Wood's fleet, and in apprehending Wood himself. In pursuance
of this policy, Henry now engaged a certain Stephen Bull, one
of his most trusted mariners, to equip three ships and to sail
north with them. Of Bull we know nothing except that he
was knighted in 1512 by Sir Edward Howard in Brittany.
His vessels duly entered the Firth of Forth in the summer of
1490, and lay in hiding behind the Isle of May, ready to pounce
out upon Wood's two famous ships, which were known to be
returning to Scotland from a voyage to Flanders, whither they
had sailed partly for commercial reasons, and partly as an escort
for another trading vessel. At length, on a sunny morning in
August, Wood's two ships hove in sight, never expecting the
presence of an enemy in the vicinity. On perceiving the English
vessels, the old Sea-Dog instantly gave battle. In the words of the
chronicler, the contest continued "fra the rising o' the sun till
the gaeing doon o' the same, in the lang simmer's day, quhile
all men and women that dwelt near the coast syd stood and beheld
the fighting, quhilk wes terrible tae sie". For three days this
naval battle continued, without intermission, during which time
the ships, interlocked, drifted to Inchcape, in the Firth of Tay.
Eventually, Wood and his Leith sailors defeated their foes, and
brought them and their vessels captive to Dundee, and later to
Leith. The only details we possess of this encounter are those
to be found in Pitscottie's picturesque record. Pitscottie, of
course, is not usually regarded as a reliable writer: as a rule, his
chronicles are taken with a grain or two of salt, except where
they are corroborated by other contemporary writers. On the
other hand, it must be remembered that he and Wood were
neighbouring lairds in Fifeshire, and that he, thus, had exceptional
opportunities for obtaining this type of information at first hand.
Furthermore, Pitscottie was a boon friend of Sir Andrew's son,
John, and also of that great Sea-Dog, Sir Robert Barton, the
first skipper of the *Great Michael*, which was launched in 1511.
It was from Barton that Pitscottie obtained all those details of
what was then the largest ship ever built, either in England or
in Scotland.

"At the last", wrote Pitscottie concerning Wood's encounter
with Stephen Bull, "upoun ane simmer morning a lytill eftir the
day breaking, ane of the Inglische schippis parsavit two schippis

command undir saill by Sancttabbis heid [St. Abbs Head] . . . .
than the captaine wes blyht and gart pearse the wyne and drank
about . . . . On the uthir syde, Schir Andrew Wode came pairtlie
forward, knawand no impediment . . . . quhill at last he persauvit
thir thrie schipis . . . . Then Andrew Wode, seand this, exortit
his men to batell . . . . lat everie man be diligent and stout for
his awin pairt and for the honour of his realm, and thairto causit
to fill the wyne and everie man drank to other. . . .

"Be this, the sun begane to ryse and schynnit bright upoun the
saillis. So the Inglischmenne apperit werie awfull in the sight of
the Scottis be resons thar schippis wes werie greit and strong and
weill furnist with greit artillye, yeit nochwithstanding the Scottis
feirit nothing, but cast thame to windwart upoun Captane Stewin
Bull and clipit together fre hand, and fought fra the sone rysing
quhill the sone yeid to, in ane lang sommer day. . . . The Scottis
men tuik curage and hardiment, and doublit thair straikis upoun
the Inglischmenne, and thair tuik Stewin Bull and his thrie
schippis and had thame up to Tay to the toun of Dondie, and
thair remaint quhill thair hurt menne wes curit and the deid
buriet."

The crews and their vessels Sir Andrew Wood handed over to
the Scottish King, who in turn presented them to King Henry,
together with the warning that thereafter Scottish waters would
be out of bounds to pirates, and that in future malefactors upon
the high seas would be treated with less clemency. To King
James, King Henry replied that "he gratefully accepted his kind-
ness, and could not but applaud the greatness of his mind".

The capture of ships by the Scottish seamen was no unusual
occurrence in those days. A few years earlier, Wood had distinguished himself by seizing the *Eagle*, a vessel that hitherto had
carried on a regular trade between England and the Netherlands,
and is referred to in Andrew Halyburton's celebrated ledger.
After Wood's time, the capture of the ships of other nationals
became almost the full-time occupation of the Bartons—the
family of Scottish Sea-Dogs that, largely single-handed, carried
on a private naval war against Portugal, which it eventually won !

The time had now arrived when it became increasingly necessary to concentrate attention upon shipbuilding and naval construction. So far as Scotland was concerned, therefore, James IV.

opened the sixteenth century with plans for making his Kingdom a sea-power of some standing among the nations. In this endeavour he sought the assistance of Wood, who now devoted his energies to the founding and development of the King's dockyards at Leith, and also at Newhaven, the *Novus Pontus*, or New Haven, of Leith.

Furthermore, he sought the expert advice of several shipwrights from Brittany and Normandy, and actually purchased a number of French ships from private owners. Toward the close of 1502, there arrived at Leith Jean Lorans, "the French wricht that cam for the schip bigging". Largely under Lorans's direction was built the good ship, *Margaret*—so named to celebrate the marriage of the Scots King and Margaret Tudor. Somewhere about 1507 was laid the keel of the *Great Michael*. In her construction the King sought advice chiefly from Sir Andrew Wood, and from Jacques Terrell, the King's master-wright, who already had won fame not only in his own country of France, but also among the maritime nations of Europe. This ship was regarded at that time as the largest in the world. So much timber was required for her that, according to Pitscottie, she demanded not only considerable consignments of timber from Norway, but she used up all the woods of Fife, with the exception of those round Falkland Palace. This is hardly surprising when we study the vessel's dimensions as set forth by the same chronicler! Her guns, for the most part, were brought from Flanders. Some of them, however, are said to have been cast at the royal forge in Edinburgh Castle. Chandeliers and the like also came from Flanders, as did her compasses, which were brought to Leith by George Paterson, another Scots Sea-Dog of this period. Denmark and her neighbours in the "Estland Seys" supplied the tar for her.

In October, 1511, the *Great Michael* was launched at Newhaven, amid great pomp and ceremony. Special trumpeters were engaged for the occasion; and there are records of additional payments having been made to the trumpeters present "at the outputting of this kingis schip". Her cost to the Scottish nation was stupendous—so stupendous that contemporary historians were in agreement that, in order to float her, all Scotland was encumbered for years. For a considerable time this leviathan lay at anchor in Leith Roads, being equipped, as the chronicler puts it, " with all manner of costly accommodation ".

The *Great Michael's* day was brief and inglorious. It seems as though this mighty vessel was beyond the seamanship of the period, since there is no record of deeds befitting such a miracle in shipbuilding.

\*   \*   \*   \*   \*

It may be mentioned in passing that in the Royal Scottish Museum at Edinburgh, and also in the Naval and Military Museum at Edinburgh Castle, one may see most beautiful models of the *Great Michael*, the *Yellow Carvel*, and other vessels sailed by the Sea-Dogs of Scotland. The scale of the model of the *Great Michael* in the Royal Scottish Museum is one inch to five feet. It shows the vessel with sails furled, and is perhaps not so gaudy as that on view in the Naval and Military Museum, portraying the ship in full sail. But both models are very beautiful indeed, and demonstrate great art and patience on the part of their makers. The model of the *Yellow Carvel* in the Royal Scottish Museum shows a typical armed merchant vessel of the late fifteenth century. The hull is carvel built. At that time the temporary fore- and stern-castles of earlier ships had given place to more permanent structures. The primary purpose of the fore-castle was still the same, namely, to provide good fighting positions for the men-at-arms; but the stern-castle (sometimes termed the summer-castle) provided deck space for the commander, and gave head-room for a cabin below.

The main-mast carried a single square sail, with a laced-on bonnet, which could be removed to shorten sail. The mizzen-mast carried a small lateen sail, which served to lighten the labour of the steersman. The original purpose of the square foresail had been to act as a head-sail; and thus the fore-mast was placed as far forward as possible.

The armament was intended to be used against the personnel only of the enemy. It consisted of seven small guns, besides culverins and cross-bows. When the ship was grappled by hooks to an enemy ship, lime-pots, fire-balls, and other missiles were thrown from the merse or fighting top.

The model is decorated in the extravagant style of the period.

The device on the mainsail is the coat-of-arms of Sir Andrew Wood, whom James III. knighted in 1483.

The year, 1512, found King James IV. supporting his ally, Louis XII., upon whom Henry VIII. had declared war. Almost the entire Scottish fleet, numbering some twenty-nine vessels, was victualled, and sailed out of the Forth in July of the following year, carrying to France no fewer than three thousand men under the command of the Earl of Arran. King James himself escorted his fleet as far as the Isle of May in order to give it encouragement, it is said, in the inevitable struggle then looming ahead. He then returned to lead his army at Flodden.

A few days after the Scottish fleet had set out for France, some of Henry's war vessels sailed northward. But they sighted none of James's ships. In order to avoid the English navy and the perils of the Straits of Dover, they had sailed round the north of Scotland, and down through the Irish Channel, to unite with the French off Brest. Some days ere his fleet reached France, King James died at Flodden. In the ensuing year peace was concluded. Scotland's vessels of war, in the main, had never even experienced an encounter with the enemy. So far as the *Great Michael* was concerned, the Duke of Albany, who represented King James at the court of Louis, sold her in 1514 to France for the meagre sum of forty thousand francs. Never again was she seen in Scottish waters. She proved of as little use to the French monarch as she had been to Scotland; and she ended her days in rotting at her mooring in the harbour of Brest.

*　　*　　*　　*　　*

All this time one family in particular was steadily coming into prominence among the mariners of Scotland; and that family was the Bartons. John Barton had three sons, each of whom has found a permanent place among the Sea-Dogs of Scotland—to wit, Andrew, the eldest, and perhaps the most celebrated; Robert, dreaded of the English, and known to them as Hob o' Barton, though affectionately called Robin in his home-port of Leith; and John, who vied with his older brothers in daring escapades at sea. All three were skilled navigators, and rendered James IV. inestimable service in the heyday of the Scottish navy. Andrew Halyburton's ledger shows that the Bartons carried on a regular trade between Leith and the Low Countries. Their fights in waters as distant as Norway and the Canaries were numerous. But it is generally conceded that their fame rests rather on the way in which they conducted a sort of private family war against Portugal, and in which they ultimately were victorious. Their difference with Portugal was one of long standing. It dated back to the year, 1476, when John Barton, the first of the family to come into the limelight in maritime affairs, was homeward bound with a cargo from Sluis, in Flanders, in his ship, the *Juliana*, and was set upon by two armed Portuguese vessels. The Scots Sea-Dog put up a good fight. But in the end the *Juliana* was captured, and Barton and his crew were thrown into one of the boats, and cast adrift. Eventually they made shore; and John Barton immediately set out for Lisbon in the hope of obtaining from the King of Portugal redress for this act of piracy, and compensation, estimated at 12,000 ducats, for the loss of his ship. Alfonso paid as little attention to his complaint as he did to the representation made on Barton's behalf by King James. Wherefore the King granted to the Barton family letters of reprisal, authorizing them to detain and appropriate any Portuguese vessels and cargoes they liked, until they considered that they had recovered the equivalent of the loss sustained by their father in the seizure of the *Juliana*. Throughout the fifteenth and sixteenth centuries, this was the customary manner of obtaining redress for acts of wanton piracy.

All three brothers now lay in wait upon the high seas for the richly laden caravels of Portugal. In their war of reprisals, several other Leith skippers joined them. Most active of the Bartons in waylaying Portuguese vessels was Andrew, into whose hands fell many enemy ships laden with precious merchandise from India. In the meanwhile, of course, the Portuguese, in like manner, sought every opportunity of retaliating on the Scottish merchant fleet, and especially on such units of it as were owned by the seamen of Leith.

Few of the Bartons' captures from the Portuguese excited so much interest in Edinburgh and Leith as did the two negro girls who, no doubt, were in course of transportation from the Guinea coast to the slave markets of America. These negresses soon became known in Scotland as " the Moorish lassies ". The Bartons

presented them as a gift to James IV., who gladly accepted them,
and showed considerable interest in their welfare. They became
maids at Edinburgh Castle to some of the ladies of the court;
and at the King's desire they were baptized and christened
Margaret and Ellen. They were well known to the Scots poet,
Dunbar, who alludes to one of them in his poem, *Ane Black-Moor*:

> *Quhen she is claid in riche apparel,*
> *She blinks as bright as ane tar barrel,*
> *My ladye with the meikle lippis.*

About this time certain Dutch ships set upon some Scottish merchant vessels, plundered them, and cast their owners
and crews adrift. In those days the owners of ships as well as the
owners of cargoes frequently sailed with them. King James
thereupon authorized Andrew Barton to visit the Dutch with
reprisals. This he did with such expedition that before long he
was sending to the King, as evidence that he had carried out his
mandate in appropriate style, several barrels full of the heads of
the Dutch pirates! Meantime his brother, Robert, or Robin,
acting in accordance with letters of marque issued by the King
himself, was despoiling the ships of Portugal in the North Sea
and the English Channel. But ill-luck befell him when, at the
instance of some Portuguese skippers, whom he had relieved of
their cargoes, the magistrates of the Dutch town of Campvere
seized his ship, the *Lion*, and sentenced him to be hanged as a
low-down pirate, unless he restored the cargoes he had taken,
or paid handsome compensation. However, news of the detention
of the *Lion* and of the fate that hung over her commander soon
reached the ears of James IV., who immediately communicated
with Margaret of Savoy, demanding that this valiant Sea-Dog,
together with his ship and crew, should be released without
delay, on the ground that his action against the Portuguese had
been authorized by the letters of marque. The result was that
both Robin and his men were set free, and the *Lion* resumed
her function upon the high seas.

In Scotland at this time, maritime insurance was almost unknown, though it had become popular in many of the maritime
towns of the Baltic and the Mediterranean. The *Lion*, therefore,
appears to have been one of the Scottish war vessels owned

jointly by the Barton family and its more intimate friends. She probably is the vessel aboard which Andrew Barton fought his last battle in the autumn of 1511. Whether she was a vessel built in France, or captured from the Portuguese, we cannot say at this distant date; but we do know that, when Sir Thomas and Sir Edward Howard captured from the Bartons a war vessel called the *Lion*, the Bartons, faithful to their tradition, simply replaced her with another war vessel of similar size and strength, which they renamed the *Lion*. We also know that, among the war fleet King James despatched to France during the Flodden campaign, there was a large vessel of war called the *Lion*, commanded by Robert Barton. On Robert's death in 1538, his great ship passed to his worthy nephew, John—worthy in that he maintained the family tradition for skilful seamanship, and prowess in face of the enemy. During the reign of Mary, Queen of Scots, the *Lion* came to grief. According to an English spy writing from Edinburgh in March, 1547, there was " great maien " (sorrow) in that city, "for a Scots ship of war, the *Lion*, wrecked near Dover with eleven score men, besides mariners ".

\*  \*  \*  \*  \*

In 1508, in pursuance of the auld alliance that had existed between the Scottish people and the Danes since the marriage of James III. with Margaret of Denmark—an alliance which greatly encouraged trading between Leith and Copenhagen—Andrew Barton sailed with two ships to assist Denmark in her commercial war with the powerful Hanseatic League. At the same time, he did not neglect to take what he could from the treasure-laden ships of Portugal, thereby increasing the resentment of the London merchants, whose trade to a large extent he now had ruined. Much as this annoyed Henry VIII., he does not seem to have made any complaint to the Scottish monarch, though it is known that he resented the way in which the Sea-Dogs of Scotland continued to outwit those of his own kingdom. And, so, nothing pleased him better than to grant the request of the Howards, that they should be permitted to equip an expedition against the Bartons, despite the fact that the merest mention of the Leith mariners literally put the fear of death on most English crews at the time. A contemporary Scottish balladist, on hearing of the design that

57

the Howards were to proceed against Andrew, records this fear by placing in the mouth of the English skipper, whom he calls Henry Hunt, the following lines :

> *Were ye but twenty ships, and he but one,*
> *I swear by kirk and bower and hall,*
> *He would o'ercome them every one,*
> *If once his beams they do downfall.*

However, the Howards came up with Andrew Barton in the Downs, as he was sailing aboard the *Lion*, which was attended by her pinnace, the *Jenny Pirwin*. Contrary to maritime practice, the English seamen displayed no ensigns on their vessels, as was the custom with war vessels, particularly in time of hostilities. Instead, they placed willow wands on the masts, " as merchants use that sayle the sea ". Though the odds were heavily against Barton, he engaged the enemy, encouraging his sailors in their death-struggle by blowing the famous whistle said to have been suspended at all times from a gold chain round his neck.

> " *Fight on, my men!* " *Sir Andrew says,*
> " *And never flinch before the foe;*
> *And stand fast by St. Andrew's Cross,*
> *As long as ye hear my whistle blow.*"

Clad in the conspicuous dress worn by the Scottish Sea-Dogs of the period, Andrew Barton was an easy target for the enemy. Early in the conflict he fell, mortally wounded. But, as long as breath remained in him, he continued to blow his whistle. When eventually the Howards' seamen boarded the *Lion*, they found its intrepid commander dead. Thus passed Andrew Barton, as he had lived. The *Lion* was now brought into the Thames by his foes. And surely it redounds to the credit of the Scottish ship-builders of the time that, at a later date, she was rechristened the *Great Harry*, and became the largest war vessel in the English fleet !

# CHAPTER FOUR

## GYPSIES OF THE BORDERLAND

QUIETLY situated among pastoral fells in the Vale of Bowmont, near the source of the Bowmont Water, and lying to all intents and purposes in the shadow of the smooth, green, sward-clad Cheviots, is the quaint Border parish and village of Yetholm—Jetham, as it used to be termed in the twelfth and thirteenth centuries. Until times comparatively recent, the remoteness of this region was proverbial. "Alike inaccessible from without, and not to be left from within" was the apt phrase used by Dr. Robert Chambers to describe Yetholm after it had lapsed into the lassitude and dreamy forgetfulness demanded by a quieter and more orderly era—an era that, following on the age-long rivalry between Scotland and England, relegated the Border feuds and forays to a romantic past.

Meandering among the Cheviot foothills, and passing by the Border keep of Graden and by Cherrytrees, there is an ancient highway leading to Yetholm and the Bowmont Water, and on, over the Border, into England. This was one of the routes so frequently adopted by invading forces throughout the centuries of Border warfare.

Strictly writing, Yetholm consists of the twin communities of Kirk-Yetholm, on the right bank of the Bowmont, and Town-Yetholm, which is placed on the left bank, and is roughly three-quarters of a mile to the west of the former. Kirk-Yetholm is within a mile and a half of the Border, whereas Town-Yetholm lies a little more than seven miles to the south-east of the historic Border town of Kelso.

The craggy face of Staerough—a spur of the Cheviots rising conspicuously on the south to an altitude of over a thousand feet above sea-level, and in some respects resembling the Salisbury Crags and Samson's Ribs in miniature—dominates both Kirk-Yetholm and Town-Yetholm. These villages are separated from England by a valley that in olden days presented a tempting means of access between the two countries, especially in time of war and baronial strife which, in the Middle Ages and, indeed, until the abolition of heritable jurisdiction, were so integral a part of the everyday life of those dwelling on the Borderland.

To-day Yetholm, embosomed in one of the many secluded dales diversifying the Cheviot Hills, is still a place forgotten and apart. Though the ubiquitous motor-bus now has established some regular contact with the outer world—with Kelso and Jedburgh on the west, with Coldstream and Berwick-on-Tweed on the north, with Wooler, in Northumberland, on the east—the parish has retained much of its pristine seclusion and aloofness. True it is, too, that the irrevocable hand of modernity has brought to Yetholm such unmistakable evidence of a new age as electric lighting and laid-on water. The grid system has actually invaded the village; and some of the more enlightened householders, encouraged by the progressive attitude of the Laird and his wife, have taken advantage of this invasion, and installed electric lighting and power in their homes. In the Border Hotel at Kirk-Yetholm, moreover, we find one of the most up-to-date hostelries in the south of Scotland. The village also boasts a bakery, replete with all the most modern mechanical equipment. Yet, though Yetholm is now so admirably situated in relation to electrical power, at night the village of pre-blackout days was still illumined by the old-fashioned paraffin lamps.

Yetholm's quaintness and picturesqueness are almost unknown to the world outside. It has been described as a little, sunny world all of its own. And such is the impression it makes upon the hill-wanderer who, perhaps for the first time, descends upon this semoted place to find its tidy cottages and emerald Green drowsing in the warmth and sunlight that, in high summer, penetrate the depths of the Cheviot valleys.

\*  \*  \*  \*  \*

Romantic, indeed, are the tales and incidents recounted in the local lore and history of Yetholm. Though the parish is pretty certain to have figured earlier than the fourteenth century, it is not until 1304 that we actually find any reliable historical reference to it. In that year the Hammer of the Scots tarried at Yetholm for a couple of days, when on his return journey to England from an expedition in the North.

Then, according to tradition long established, the kirk at Kirk-Yetholm shares with the little, grey kirk at Southdean (or Souden) near Hawick, the distinction of having been the rendezvous of a section of the Scottish army that in 1388, under the leadership of the intrepid Earl of Douglas, routed the English at the Battle of Otterburn, or Chevy Chase. The actual place of assembly of Douglas's forces, however, was the kirk at Southdean. Here the Scots nobles held secret and decisive council of war before marching forth to give battle on English soil.

Six miles or so to the east of Yetholm lies Flodden Field, where James IV. and his invading army suffered defeat at the hands of the English, under Surrey. The tradition that the remains of many of the Scottish nobility, vanquished on that fateful field, were carried back into Scotland, and interred in the kirk and kirkyard at Yetholm, is still retained tenaciously throughout the Borderland. The kirk at Kirk-Yetholm was the nearest consecrated spot to Flodden on Scottish soil; and the fallen were conveyed hither that they might rest in the land of their fathers, when the flowers o' the forest were a' wede-awa'.

About the year, 1832, a stone coffin, containing a skeleton of unusual size, was found in the kirk, some six feet below the level of the floor. Shortly afterwards, when digging operations were being carried out in the kirkyard, there was discovered a square erection consisting of four rough stones set at right angles, and covered by a slab. It contained only a skull, which crumbled to dust when exposed to the atmosphere. It is supposed that the skeleton and skull were the remains of a chieftain who fell at Flodden.

Tradition also has it—and probably with some degree of justification—that in 1745 a small band of Highlanders, faithful adherents of Prince Charlie, marched through the parish and village of Yetholm, and by the Vale of Bowmont, to Earl, in Northumberland. It had been arranged that here they would receive certain sums of money remitted from France to aid them in their cause. The money was placed in the custody of one, Charles Selby, Esquire, of Earl. A century and a quarter ago, there died at Yetholm a very old man, whom the villagers often recalled long after he had passed on, because he was supposed to have seen the Highlanders march past the door of his father's cottage, when on their way south toward London.

★   ★   ★   ★   ★

Yetholm's chief interest, however, lies in the fact that, for generations, it was the headquarters of the Scottish Gypsies, or at any rate of the largest colony of them. There still may be seen at Kirk-Yetholm the Palace occupied by the Gypsy 'royal family' —the place of residence of the Kings and Queens, of the Princes and Princesses, of Gypsydom. Even to-day one is able to recognize about Yetholm and its green loanings the dark eyes and swarthy countenance of the Romany, although fifty years have passed by since the coronation on the village Green of Yetholm of the last King of the Gypsies, and there are now dwelling in this locality few of pure Gypsy stock. When Borrow visited the Scottish Gypsies, he was told by one of them that Yetholm had been their centre " beyond the memory of man ", but that the name of Faa was " clean dead in the land, though there was some of the blood remaining ".

It is believed that the Gypsies first came to Scotland about the middle of the fifteenth century. At that time, and for a considerable period thereafter, they were known throughout the land as the Saracens. Tradition asserts that a band of them had committed extensive depredations in Galloway during the reign of James II. of Scotland, who, as you will remember, was killed at the siege of Roxburgh Castle in 1460. But the earliest record we appear to have of these wanderers within our realm is an entry in the Book of the Lord High Treasurer. It runs as follows : "Apr. 22, 1505—Item to the Egyptianis be the Kingis command, vij. lib."

Then, we know that on July, 5th, of the ensuing year, Anthonius Gawino, who is described as the Earl of Little Egypt, received from James IV. letters commending him to the King of Denmark, for which country this Gypsy chief was on the point of taking ship.

In 1540 James V. entered into some sort of bargain with the Gypsy potentate, John Faa. On the 15th of February of that year, King James subscribed a letter, under the Privy Seal of Scotland, in favour of "oure louit Johnne Faw, Lord and Erle of

62

Litill Egipt ". The Faws, or Faas, were among the earliest and most powerful Gypsy settlers at Yetholm; and, as we shall see later, they were the Royal House among the Romany in Scotland.

★    ★    ★    ★    ★

It is impossible to fix with any degree of accuracy the date at which these wandering tribes first settled in the south of Scotland. Many hold that they came to Yetholm in 1449, the year of the passing of the Act aforementioned. But Border tradition asserts that the Gypsies did not become established at Yetholm until the close of the seventeenth century, when "a peculiar people", not too prone to good works, was permitted to take up residence in the locality. It happened—so the tradition continues—that at the siege of Namur, in 1695, one of their race saved the life of Captain David Bennet, proprietor of the Barony of Grubbit, on which were situated both Kirk-Yetholm and Town-Yetholm. While mounting a breach, Captain Bennet was felled to the ground. All his comrades were slain with the exception of a Gypsy named Young, who, with conspicuous gallantry, rescued his officer, and then climbed the parapet and seized the flag. This act so inspired the besiegers, it is said, that they renewed their assault, consolidated their position in the breach, and finally took Namur. In recognition of the Gypsy's succour and valour, Captain Bennet is believed to have erected the cottages at Yetholm, and to have granted perpetual leases of them to members of the Gypsy tribe at a nominal quit rental.

According to an interesting brochure published by a certain Robert Murray in 1875, entitled *The Gypsies of the Border*, and dedicated to "Her Majesty, Esther Faa Blythe, the Gypsy Queen", a different explanation is given of their coming to Yetholm. Murray tells us that, during ' The Fifteen ', a contingent of the Jacobite army passed up the Vale of Bowmont on its way to England, and that these adherents to the Stuart cause levied the support of themselves upon the inhabitants as they marched along, pressing man and horse into the service of that unfortunate dynasty. Now, it so happened that one of their number made off with a valuable horse from the estate of Marlfield, the property of Sir William Bennet. So infuriated by this act was the baronet, we are told, that he straightway engaged a Gypsy, vagrant in

63

the neighbourhood, to recover the stolen animal. The Gypsy immediately followed the Jacobites. Under cover of darkness, he crept stealthily through their encampment, released the horse from its tether, and rode back with him to Marlfield. As a reward for this service, Sir William bestowed upon the Gypsy a house in Kirk-Yetholm; and it is said that, from the time he and his family took up residence there, the Gypsy tribes of Scotland have made Kirk-Yetholm their headquarters, and the place of their abode during the months of the year that the inclemency of the weather precluded them from their characteristic wanderings.

It is unimportant from our point of view which version of the Gypsies' coming to Yetholm is the true one. What we do know is that Mr. Nisbet of Dirleton, who succeeded to Captain Bennet's properties, accepted the rôle of his predecessor as patron of the Gypsies dwelling at Kirk-Yetholm, and whimsically alluded to the male members of their tribe as his bodyguard.

★   ★   ★   ★   ★

Yetholm is typical of the kind of country in which the Scottish Gypsies have been located throughout the centuries. These tribes of wanderers seem to have had a partiality for settling on the fringe of low, fertile, populous country with a background of inaccessible hills and valleys, or of moorland or impenetrable swamp, to which they might readily retire out of reach when harassed or pursued by the authorities. In such respects all the well-known Gypsy haunts in Scotland bear a resemblance to one another—Biggar, in Lanarkshire, for example; Lochmaben, in Dumfries; Lochgelly, in Fife; Greenlaw and Gordon, in Berwickshire; and Middleton, in Midlothian.

There was also a considerable Gypsy settlement in Peeblesshire. At Romanno Bridge, in that county, was fought one of the most sanguinary feuds recorded in the annals of these vagabonds. On October, 1st, 1677, two Gypsy clans, the Shaws and the Faas, returning from the Haddington Fair, and on their way to Harestanes to meet two other Gypsy clans, the Browns and the Baillies, with whom they were at enmity, came to high words over the sharing of the haul they had taken at Haddington. High words came to blows; and before long blows came to knives.

The Cheviots from the road to Mindrum, with Kirk-Yetholm in the middle-distance

Kirk-Yetholm from the slopes of Staerough

Town-Yetholm and the Cheviot Fells from the slopes of Staerough in midsummer

The Gypsy Palace at Kirk-Yetholm

Where the road to England leaves Scotland at the Green o' Kirk-Yetholm

Esther Faa.
Late Queen of Yetholm Gipsies

*Photo by Gibson, Coldstream*

Queen Esther Faa, with the Gypsy Sword of State

*Photo by Gibson, Coldstream*

Coronation at Kirk-Yetholm in 1898 of King Charles II, on his accession to the Gypsy Throne occupied by his late mother, Queen Esther Faa. He wears the Gypsy crown and holds the Sword of State

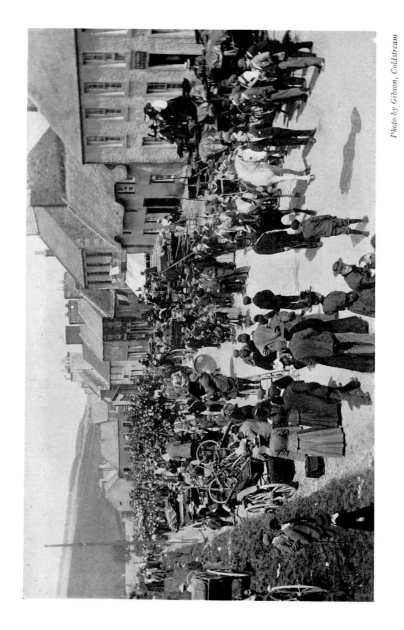

*Photo by Gibson, Coldstream*

Coronation Day at Town-Yetholm—Whit Monday, 1898, when the Gypsy King, Charles II, was crowned

Apart from the many womenfolk attached to both factions, on the Shaws' side there were Robin Shaw and his three sons: on the Faas' side four brethren and a brother's son. In the mêlée that developed, the Faas were routed. Old Sandy Faa, "a bold and proper fellow", and his wife were killed on the spot, while Geordie Faa was seriously wounded. At the Grassmarket of Edinburgh, in February, 1678, old Robin Shaw and his sons were hanged for their evil-doing at Romanno. Some days later one of the surviving Faas was hanged likewise for another murder.

An interesting reference to this Gypsy battle is to be found in Lord Fountainhall's MS., now preserved in the National Library of Scotland. The Browns and the Baillies, it appears, had come over from Ireland some little time previously; and certain Scottish tribes, resentful of their arrival, had decided to chase them back.

In 1683 Dr. Alexander Pennicuik, on whose estate this "memorable polymachy" occurred, erected a dovecot on the site, and inscribed the following lines on its lintel:

*A.D. 1683.*
*The field of Gipsie blood, where here you see,*
*A shelter for the harmless dove shall be.*

The clothed remains of the four hanged Shaws were cast into a hole purposely dug for them in Greyfriars' Kirkyard, at Edinburgh. But on the following morning the corpse of the youngest of them, who was barely sixteen, could not be found. "Some thought", writes Lord Fountainhall, "that being last thrown over the ladder and first cut down, and in full vigour, and not much earth placed upon him, and lying uppermost, and so not so ready to smother, the fermentation of the blood and heat of the bodies under him might cause him to rebound and throw off the earth, and recover ere the morning and steal away, which, if true, he deserved his life, though the magistrates deserved a reprimand. But others, more probably, thought his body was stolen away by some chirurgeon or his servant, to make an anatomical dissection on."

The hanging of Gypsies was no uncommon occurrence in Scotland about this time. On the Dule Tree, or tree of sorrow, growing beside the ancient tower of Cassillis, the sixth Earl of

Cassillis hanged no fewer than fifteen Gypsies in revenge for Johnnie Faa's having eloped with his wife. Johnnie was one of the best known Border Gypsies of his day. He and his unfortunate followers met their end with the Earl's wife as witness. This gruesome act has found permanent commemoration in *The Gypsy Laddie*, a Border Ballad, of which the following verse is typical:

> *They were fifteen valiant men,*
> *Black, but very bonnie;*
> *And they all lost their lives for ane—*
> *The Earl o' Cassillis' lady.*

★　　★　　★　　★　　★

Obviously, at no time is an accurate census of a wandering people very practicable. At the close of the eighteenth century the Gypsy population of Kirk-Yetholm was estimated at 50. By 1818 the colony had increased to 109. Twenty years later, however, it had decreased to approximately 100. By 1846 it again appears to have risen to 140. In 1862 no more than 126 Gypsies were to be found in the parish of ·Yetholm. When Robert Murray of Hawick paid his visit to the Kingdom of the Gypsies in 1875, he found it to consist of eighteen families, ten bearing the name of Douglas, four that of Blythe, two that of Tait, one that of Ruthven, and one that of Rutherford. At that time the Faa tribe, from whom the Monarch of the Gypsies used to be chosen, was extinct in the male line, as was also the tribe of Youngs.

A decade or so after Murray's visit, the Gypsy population had dwindled to 45. It comprised thirteen families, together with five persons known not to have been of pure Gypsy stock. The Douglas clan was the most numerous among them; and it is said that, when the colony turned out to the annual football match on Fastern E'en—Shrove Tuesday—the Douglases were readily distinguishable from the rest of this dark-countenanced people because most of them were in-kneed. This tribal characteristic was attributed to the fact that for generations they roamed about the country on horseback, while other contingents of their fraternity moved about in caravans or on foot.

The Gypsies, throughout their long residence ·at Yetholm,

married and intermarried almost exclusively among their own race; and it was regarded as remarkable that, despite this intensive inbreeding over at least a century and a half, cases of imbecility among them were extremely rare. Very occasionally external blood was introduced when a roving Borderer, following a Gypsy tribe for years and identifying himself with its pursuits, at length was received into the family, and perhaps found an indulgent Gypsy mother-in-law. But such instances were quite exceptional. Even more exceptional were cases where Gypsy women contracted marriages outside their own race. What is equally interesting is that, in all such cases, the outsider marrying a Gypsy bride or bridegroom invariably entered the Gypsy home, and adopted its manners and customs. One instance of an extra-tribal matrimonial alliance is still spoken of in Yetholm. A member of the Douglas tribe enlisted in King George's army as a substitute during the French War, at a time when a bounty of as much as fifty or sixty guineas was paid to substitutes by timid farmers and other well-to-do members of the community who happened to have been balloted for the militia. While stationed at Durham, Douglas, representing himself to be the son of a wealthy Scottish farmer, married the daughter of a local merchant. When, in course of time, he obtained his discharge, and brought his Durham wife home to Yetholm, she was soon disillusioned at finding the family donkey standing by the door of the shack occupied by her father-in-law. Part of the shack was the donkey's stable. Instead of exhibiting the rage and resentment that such deception might have justified, she quietly accepted her fate. She lived out her days in Gypsydom, probably as contentedly as if she had married the mayor of her home town. Throughout the Borderland she went by the name of Durham Mary. At Kirk-Yetholm she bore her Gypsy husband a family, which afterwards moved to Hawick, and ultimately emigrated to America.

\* \* \* \* \*

Among the more illustrious of the Gypsy 'royal family' dwelling at Kirk-Yetholm was Old Will Faa, who is said to have been the first real King of the Yetholm Gypsies, and who was known throughout the countryside as Glee'd-Neckit Wull, because of the twist in his neck. Old Will Faa claimed that he was the direct lineal descendant of the very John Faa, Lord and Earl of Little Egypt, who, along with his tribe, was given recognition and protection under the hand and seal of King James V. He was acknowledged as King not only of the Borderland Gypsies, but also of all the Romany tribes roaming over the north of England and the north of Scotland. He was thrice married; and his wives bore him no fewer than twenty-four children. He appeared at each of the christenings in his wedding robes. Every christening was the occasion for great pomp and ceremony. A royal retinue of twelve young handmaids waited upon the numerous guests assembled either to witness the ceremony, or to indulge themselves during the festivity that followed. The guests at the christenings of the children of King William I., as Old Will Faa was entitled, usually included the neighbouring lairds and farmers, with whom he continued on amicable terms. The Murrays of Cherrytrees and the Nisbets of Dirleton, for example, were usually present on such occasions. Nisbet of Dirleton remained one of the Gypsy King's most beneficent patrons. When the King learned that Mr. Nisbet was lying seriously ill at his family seat in East Lothian (a seat that at the time of the Gowrie Conspiracy was described by Logan of Restalrig as the " pleasantest dwelling in Scotland "), he set off on foot from Yetholm, though over eighty years of age, that he might see his benefactor before he died. On his way through Kelso, he called at the house of Baillie Smith, Mr. Nisbet's factor, to inform him of the venture upon which he was bent. In those days there were no trains, of course ; and the stage coaches serving the Borderland were few and far between. In any case, it is questionable whether Old Will would have been beholden to any such mode of transport, even had it been available, for he was a man of great independence, preferring Shank's Mare to anything that moved on wheels. In record time he reached Dirleton, where the sick laird received him hospitably, and replenished his purse. Thereafter he strode on to Edinburgh. Never before had he seen the Scottish Capital during the four-score years of his life ; and it occurred to him that an additional twenty miles or thereby to his itinerary might be justified in correcting this omission. On the market-day following his arrival at Edinburgh, he chanced to meet on the

North Bridge some Border farmers whom he knew, in whose presence he gleefully tossed his old, brown hat in the air, boasting the while that he had tramped all the way from Yetholm to Dirleton, and had arrived there just in time to speak with the dying laird. When returning home by the east coast, this first acknowledged King of the Scottish Gypsies suddenly fell ill at Coldingham. There he died in 1784.

News of his death soon reached his Kingdom, and spread rapidly amongst the Gypsy tribes dwelling on both sides of the Border. Several hundred Gypsies frae a' the airts convened at the ancient village of Coldingham to form the funeral train that brought his remains home to Kirk-Yetholm for burial. Along the entire route of thirty miles, groups of townsfolk and villagers gathered to pay their last homage to the dead King, and to witness a procession that, with no fewer than three hundred asses, must have been reminiscent of patriarchal times. Thus Old Will Faa was given a 'royal' funeral; and it is said that, after his remains were committed to earth, the inhabitants of Yetholm feasted in pagan style for three days and three nights.

*    *    *    *    *

On the demise of the Glee'd-Neckit monarch, his son, William II., commonly known throughout the Borderland as Wull Faa, and now a man of thirty-three years of age, ascended the throne, but not without encountering opposition. There was a rival claimant to the Gypsy Crown. The death of 'Auld Wull', therefore, was followed by an outbreak of something in the nature of civil war among the Gypsies. However, the majority of them regarded the rival claimant as a usurper who, having taken a mean advantage of the sorrow and confusion occasioned by the death of the late King, had seized the reins of state by violence, and in like manner sought to retain them. The rival was actually the chief of an inferior tribe, to which position he had succeeded on the death of his father, a man so notorious for his evil-doing as to have earned for himself the soubriquet of the Earl of Hell—indeed, a man who is said to have rubbed shoulders with the gallows on at least one occasion. On the Green o' Kirk-Yetholm the factions ultimately came face to face; and there ensued a battle-royal in which the Faa forces were victorious, and after which Will Faa was proclaimed William II., King of the Gypsies, in succession to his worthy father, 'Auld Wull'.

King William was a man distinguished for his strength and prowess. He had gained some distinction as a prize-fighter: he was looked upon as a veritable Samson. When obliged to abandon tent life during the cold months of winter, he eked out a livelihood by carting coals, either to Kelso or to Jedburgh, from the mine at a place called Etal.

During his reign the clandestine traffic in exciseable commodities between Scotland and England was at its zenith. Smuggling had always been one of the main occupations of the Borderers; and it is estimated that about this time roughly a fifth of the population of the twin communities of Kirk-Yetholm and Town-Yetholm was directly engaged in it. In fact, the comparative backwardness of Yetholm up till about the middle of last century was attributed, firstly, to the non-residence of the proprietors, and, secondly, to the illegal practice, so firmly established and so widely prevalent in the neighbourhood, of smuggling whisky across the Border. While King William reigned at Yetholm, Scottish whisky to the value of £20,000 was sold in his Kingdom for consumption in England, while quantities of rum and gin were smuggled simultaneously from the coast into Scotland. Considerable supplies of these liquors were landed secretly at such small ports on the Northumberland coast as Boulmer, and then carried through the Border hills to Yetholm for distribution.

It was only natural that a man of Will Faa's temperament should have had a considerable hand in this smuggling business. The drinks themselves, together with the handsome profits obtainable from so risky a traffic, made an appeal to him wellnigh irresistible. The penalties awaiting those caught in this trade were, indeed, severe; but, to Will Faa's way of thinking, the profits accruing were well worth the risks involved. However, on one occasion he fell foul of the gaugers, or excisemen. He was returning on horseback to Yetholm from Boulmer with a couple of kegs of Holland gin, when he encountered a party of excise officials, one of whom was mounted, and armed with a sword. Against this formidable array of authority, poor Will had no weapon but an oak cudgel. So he tried to escape. In order that his flight should be as little encumbered as possible, he cut the twine binding the kegs to the saddle. A desperate chase now ensued, in which Will probably would have outwitted his pursuer, had he not ventured to evade him by diverting through a boggy field in which his mount stuck fast. The gauger, now close on his heels, dismounted, and proceeded toward him, sword in hand. Against the swordsmanship of his adversary, Will's poor cudgel proved of little account, dexterously though he handled it. In the duel that followed, the cudgel was soon hacked to pieces. But the Gypsy fought on until the exciseman's sword, having fallen heavily upon his right hand, compelled him to surrender. As he abandoned the contest, he remarked that his opponent had damaged what, by common consent, was the most skilful bow hand in Scotland—a reference to his acknowledged proficiency as a fiddler!

Will was landlord of 'The Queen' in Kirk-Yetholm. During the latter years of his reign, he is said to have assumed the habit of the sporting gentleman, wearing a velveteen jacket and a white hat covered with fly-hooks of every size and hue, and suitable for all weathers and waters. No one in all the wide Borderland was better acquainted with the streams of Teviotdale than he: his knowledge of the lurking-places of the finny tribe was proverbial.

Among King William's more strenuous pastimes was football. On the haugh at Town-Yetholm, by the left bank of the Bowmont Water, there was played every Fastern E'en a football match between the married and the single men of Yetholm. Until his lithe limbs began to stiffen with advancing years, Will took a prominent part in this match. He was looked upon as one of the finest footballers of his time; and for close on three-quarters of a century he and his tribe turned out to participate in, or witness, this annual contest. The game continued until darkness obliged the players to abandon it for the conviviality of the seven or eight inns then to be found in the district. There they and their supporters ate and drank and danced until daybreak.

King William Faa II. reigned over the Gypsies until 1847. In October of that year he died at the age of ninety-six. From ailments of the body he never suffered in any way, though he used to contend that he found himself more liable to colds when living in a house than when living in a tent.

✷   ✷   ✷   ✷   ✷

Now, since Will had neither son nor daughter to succeed him, the crown was conferred upon his brother-in-law, Charlie Blythe. Charlie was by no means a young man when he ascended the throne. For all that, he retained much of the vigour and alertness of his early manhood. Than his predecessors, he was, maybe, less illiterate. He could read tolerably well; and from observation and conversation he had amassed a considerable amount of information of one kind or another. It is still said of him in Yetholm that, after the crown had been placed upon his head, he flourished the royal sword in the presence of his subjects, and exclaimed: "King I am; and King I shall remain!"

There were few in the Borderland so well versed in the Border Ballads as was King Charlie Blythe. He numbered among the friends of his earlier years Sir Walter Scott, with whom he frequently conversed. Scott often sauntered along to visit him when he pitched his tent at a certain spot near Abbotsford, during his seasonal wanderings. It may be mentioned in this connection that Scott derived much for his writings from the contacts he had made with the Yetholm Gypsies. Indeed, Jean Gordon, a Gypsy born at Kirk-Yetholm about 1670, is believed to have been the prototype of Meg Merrilees, of whom we read in *Guy Mannering*.

King Charlie often bewailed his lot as that of a monarch whose monarchy provided him with no revenue. For all that, he never allowed himself to forget that he was King of the Gypsies, and that this distinction demanded of him certain high standards in matters of conduct and bearing. Despite the complete absence of revenue from his subjects, his Palace at Kirk-Yetholm was no mean dwelling. Tourists from all parts of the United Kingdom called upon him there, and learned of his Gypsy lineage and heritage. In his declining years he derived some measure of comfort from the gifts sent to him from time to time by visitors to the Gypsy Palace. He was an inveterate reader of the Bible, and equally inveterate chewer of tobacco. For the latter he seldom wanted: his visitors supplied him adequately.

King Charlie died at Yetholm in 1861, at the age of eighty-three, having reigned peacefully for fourteen years. Now his son, David Blythe, would have succeeded to the throne in his stead, had he not waived his claim in favour of his youngest sister, Princess Helen, bynamed Black-bearded Nell. But Esther, the eldest sister, protested against this settlement of the succession, not merely on the strength of her seniority, but also on the ground that she carried the royal name of Faa—her full name was Esther *Faa* Blythe. Determined not to be removed from the throne by a mere usurper in the person of her sister, Esther issued the following proclamation :

"I, Esther Faa Blythe, hereby notify and make known that, in consequence of the lamented death of my father, lately reigning King of the Gypsies, and in consequence of a pretender to the vacant crown having arisen in the person of my youngest sister, the question in dispute will be settled at Yetholm, on Tuesday, the twelfth day of November instant ; and I do hereby summon and command all the members of the various tribes to appear there on the day named, and at the same time invite all the neighbours favourable to my cause to come forward and record their votes in my favour, by doing which they will ensure the promotion to royal honours and authority of the candidate possessing the most rightful claim, bearing, as I do, the royal name of Faa, and being the eldest daughter of his late Majesty, King Charles, and earn the endearing gratitude of my royal heart.

ESTHER FAA BLYTHE.

"Given under my hand and seal this day of November in the Year of our Lord, eighteen hundred and sixty-one years."

But Esther still had to contend against her sister and the noisy faction supporting that Princess's claim. It was argued that Helen had the right to succeed because her late father, King Charlie, had expressed such a desire on his death-bed, because she had nursed the old King in his failing years, and because he had made over to her all his worldly possessions. Notwithstanding, Helen herself was none too sure of her claim to the throne. But she placed great reliance on the fact that she was now the sole owner and occupier of the Gypsy Palace. When she went on a visit to another Gypsy court, presumably in the hope of meeting a valiant knight who would do battle for her and her kingdom, she barricaded the door and windows of the royal residence (at that time a humble, one-storey, thatched cabin with a wooden paling in front of it) lest her rival sister should attempt to take possession of it by force. When Esther learned of her royal sister's absence from Yetholm, she quickly appeared on the scene, and started a personal canvass of the community. By this device she completely gained the support of her tribe. So, it was decided that the matter of the succession should be put to the popular vote. However, on Fastern E'en, the day appointed for the polling, the rival claimant failed to enter an appearance; and Esther, therefore, was able to sustain her claim without opposition. Wherefore, on November, 19th, 1861, she was solemnly proclaimed Queen of the Gypsies. Attended by the Princes and Princesses of Gypsydom, and mounted on her palfrey, Her Majesty proceeded to the Cross of Yetholm, followed by the crown-bearer and the crowner. There the coronation ceremony was performed, in presence of a great assembly. Reading from a scroll, the crowner first declared his right to officiate on this occasion, because he had placed the same crown upon the head of her late father, King Charles. He then duly crowned her, and proclaimed her Queen Esther Faa Blythe, "challenge who dare!" The Queen, in a brief and pathetic speech, responded to the cheers that went up from those who had placed her so handsomely on the throne of her ancestors. She expressed the hope that, during her reign, her subjects would be peace-loving and law-abiding. A generous supply of 'mountain-dew' was then handed round, and the assembly drank heartily to Her Majesty's health and happiness. Thereafter the procession was re-formed. Headed by the Queen's piper, who was mounted on his charger, it set out on a tour of the village inns. This was followed by a dance on the Green o' Kirk-Yetholm. But the coming of rain toward the close of day damped more than the enthusiasm of the dancers; and, so, the dance had to be abandoned untimeously. Coronation Day was concluded by Queen Esther's holding a 'drawing-room' at the Palace.

Queen Esther was a woman of fiery temper; and, when her blood was up, she was capable of displaying remarkable eloquence. It is said that she neither laid claim to possessing the second-sight, nor indulged to excess her profession of fortune-telling. Yet, she was widely known for her practice in the arts of the spae-wife.

$$\star \quad \star \quad \star \quad \star \quad \star$$

For all the Palace and royal titles, Queen Esther Faa Blythe at various periods in her life was visited by penury. In March, 1867, six years after she had ascended the throne, application for assistance was made on her behalf to the Jedburgh Parochial Board, on the ground that Jedburgh was the place of settlement of John Rutherford, her late husband, who was known throughout the Borderland as Jethart Jock. From information placed at the disposal of the Board, the Queen then possessed a pony and trap, with which she used to wander through the land. Eight of her twelve children were alive; and all but one of the eight were married and had children. As none of her relatives appeared to be able or inclined to support her, the Board generously offered to admit her to the county poorhouse. But would the proud Esther accept such charity? Not a bit of her! On the contrary, she deemed it improper that the authorities should have made so unseemly an offer to a descendant of the Royal House of Faa!

Like King Charlie before her, she was inordinately fond of tobacco. But, whereas the King chewed most of the tobacco presented to him, his queenly daughter preferred to stuff it into her small, black cutty. This Gypsy Queen, when on her tribal wanderings, wore a scarlet robe of state, a purple hood, sometimes a purple jacket, and elastic-sided boots. She was fairer in complexion than any of her swarthy subjects. I have been told by those who knew her that she was " a canny, auld budie, who had little of the Romany in her face or language ". She preferred Kirk-Yetholm to Town-Yetholm. The former, she used to explain, " has the parish kirk; Kirk-Yetholm has the mill; and Kirk-Yetholm has *me* ". Latterly she believed herself to be the only genuine Gypsy in all the countryside.

She was very proud of her tin crown, regarding it, as did her royal ancestors, as the most precious of her possessions. When asked, as she frequently was, why her subjects could not get together, and subscribe toward a more elaborate and expensive crown, she derived satisfaction from replying that, so far as she was concerned, a tin crown answered the purpose every bit as well as a golden one would have done. On one occasion she was persuaded to lend the Gypsy crown to an exhibition at the Border town of Hawick. There this emblem of regality received such rough treatment that it had to be repaired. The Gypsy

sword of state also figured at this time among the exhibits at
Hawick. This sword the royal Faas were believed to have taken
from their adversaries in a Border raid, centuries earlier. When
lent, it bore the date, 332! But, after the exhibition, it was
left lying about in Hawick for some months, with the result that
it had to be cleaned, in the process of which the date became
obliterated. The sword, as a rule, was suspended from the ceiling
of Queen Esther's living-room in the Palace. So, too, was a
horse-pistol she prized.

Perhaps the most pleasing account of Queen Esther is that
which appeared in *Chambers's Journal* in 1883, shortly after her
death. Four months earlier, its author had visited Yetholm
"especially for the purpose of introducing a friend to Esther Faa
Blythe, the Queen of the Gypsies", then in her eighty-first year.
To her visitors on this occasion Queen Esther described Yetholm
in words that since have become proverbial throughout the
Borderland. " Yetholm", she declared, "is sae mingle-mangle
that ane micht think it was built on a dark nicht, or sawn [sown]
on a windy ane." By this time, however, the parish had lost
much of its picturesqueness and quaintness. Most of the old,
thatched cottages forming the Tinklers' Row had disappeared.
The Royal Palace, then occupied by the Queen herself, was a
detached, whitewashed cottage of more modern appearance.
A flower-plot graced the front of it; and ivy clung to its gables.
It was comfortable within, though perhaps humble. The Queen
moved about her royal residence with an air of dignity and
courteousness, showing her guests the most interesting objects
it contained. Among such objects was the Gypsy regalia. This
consisted of the tin crown made by a Yetholm blacksmith named
George Gladstone, the sword of state, and a sword picked up at
Flodden Field. Queen Esther took great pride in exhibiting
these heirlooms to those who came to see her at the Palace; and
she also derived no small satisfaction from showing her visitors
the many precious rings and kindred keepsakes presented to her
by interested and wealthy visitors who had found their way
to Kirk-Yetholm during her reign.

In conversation she was wont to bemoan the changes that had
taken place in the parish, and had affected her subjects so dis-
advantageously. The Police Acts she regarded as unnecessarily

stringent. Though she claimed to be a strict observer of the law, she recognized the difficulties confronting the Gypsy race when police regulations obliged its members to abandon habits they had inherited, or had acquired in childhood. In her declining years, she ruefully maintained that the inhabitants of Yetholm were "maistly Irish, and nane o' ma ain seed, breed, and generation".

Queen Esther Faa Blythe ruled over Little Egypt from 1861 until 1883. On July, 12th, of the latter year, she died in a house at Kelso known as the Castle. Here she had taken up residence some years previously. At first it was arranged that her remains should be interred at Kelso. However, to the satisfaction of the countryside, they were borne to Kirk-Yetholm. There they were committed on Sunday, 15th, beside the graves in which moulders the dust of her husband and her parents and other members of her kindred. Her grave lies literally within calling distance of the Palace, in which she spent the happiest years of her life, and from which she reigned over her people with a considerable degree of acceptance. Her coffin bore the inscription:

ESTHER FAA BLYTHE

QUEEN OF THE GYPSIES

Died July, 12, 1883.

On the bier were strewn flowers and evergreens, and a wreath of white roses from Lady John Scott of Spottiswoode. Large crowds followed the hearse out of Kelso; and the streets between the Castle and Kelso Bridge were lined with hundreds of onlookers. Clusters of rural folk gathered at various points all along the roadside, eager to witness the Queen's coffin bearing her for the last time to Kirk-Yetholm. It was estimated that at Kirk-Yetholm no fewer than fifteen hundred people awaited the cortège. Mourners had come from places as distant as Carlisle and Berwick-on-Tweed. On the coffin's arrival at the entrance to the kirkyard, it was draped with the royal cloak and scarlet cloth worn for so many years by the late Queen. Male representatives of the Yetholm people now shouldered it to the grave prepared for it at the east end of the kirkyard, where it was lowered in presence of a great concourse. But it is said that among the multitude there were few of the swarthy race paying their final tribute—perhaps, twenty-five in all.

*　*　*　*　*

With the passing of Queen Esther, the throne became vacant. It was not until Whit Monday, 1898, that her eldest son, Prince Charles—Charles Faa Blythe, to give him his full name—was crowned Charles II., King of the Gypsies, on the historic Green o' Kirk-Yetholm. King Charles's coronation created a great stir in the Borderland. He was seventy years of age when he came to the throne and first flourished the sword of state he had inherited from his mother. But he was a man of considerable vivacity, for all his years; and, forby, he was an acceptable representative of the Gypsy dynasty, in that his complexion was swarthy, and he exhibited several other racial characteristics of which the Gypsies were proud. King Charles had been a rover all his days. In the old coaching times he used to hire himself out by the half-year. When the railways were developing in the north of England, he obtained fairly steady employment. Later he went to Alnwick, where he was engaged on bridge work by the factor to the Duke of Northumberland. He had settled down at Kirk-Yetholm only a couple of years before he was invited to accept the crown of his ancestors. "I hereby crown Charles Faa Blythe as King of the Gypsies, wherever they be, challenge who dare", declared the hereditary crowner in placing the crown upon his head; "and I summon all his loyal people to do him homage and respect. Long live the King!"

Prior to his having had this distinction thrust upon him, he and his wife were keeping a common lodging-house at Yetholm. They both were people of good character; and it was with a view to putting them into more comfortable and easy circumstances in their declining years, as well as to preserve the Gypsy rule, that this coronation movement was inaugurated. A certain Mr. Govanlock, to whom the Gypsy Palace belonged at the time, had had the cottage done up for their reception.

King Charles II. did not reign long. Death bore away this Gypsy Monarch in 1902; and the throne of the Romany Kingdom has been without an occupant ever since. He was the last of the Gypsy hierarchy to wear the tin crown, and to wield the Gypsy sword of state.

★   ★   ★   ★   ★

No account of the Gypsies of the Borderland would be complete without some reference to the life and labours of the Rev. John Baird, who was ordained minister of Yetholm in 1829. When Baird came to the parish, its church was low-lying, damp, and thatched, its manse uninhabitable to all intents and purposes. The eminence upon which the manse stood resembled a wilderness. Furthermore, the sole means of communication between the two communities of Town-Yetholm and Kirk-Yetholm was a footbridge, narrow and wooden, and carried away by spates at least once every year. At this time, too, the proclivities of the Gypsies had lent to the district a notoriety none too enviable. In such a parish was Mr. Baird's lot cast. But he immediately set himself to rectify all these defects—and, in particular, to reclaim the Gypsies by breaking down their indolent and vagabond habits, and by bringing them within the ambit of ordinary society. The heritors repaired and enlarged the manse; while the minister himself, anxious to contribute what he could to the amenities of his parish, selected for his labours the gravelly bank falling steeply to the haugh below, levelled out the bank's asperities, and planted it with trees. A substantial and commodious church was then built to replace the old, thatched one which, in the meantime, had been pulled down. In 1834 the wooden bridge was removed, and the two townships became united by a solid, three-arched bridge, sufficiently wide to admit of the free passage of carts and carriages.

Meanwhile Baird was giving serious consideration to the problem of how best he could redeem the wayward Gypsies, who were being regarded by many of the more enlightened as evidence of the fulfilment of the ancient prophecy contained in the Book of Ezekiel: "I will scatter the Egyptians among the nations, and disperse them through the countries". Did not the Gypsies style themselves the Lords and Earls of Little Egypt, and crown their rulers Kings of Little Egypt?

Within eighteen months of his coming to Yetholm, Baird had devised a scheme for the reforming of the Gypsies. He was considerably encouraged when he observed that many of them were beginning to attend church regularly, and that the attendance at the Sabbath School was increasing correspondingly. About this time there was formed in Edinburgh a society, the sole purpose of which was the reformation of the Scottish Gypsies. The committee of this society selected Kirk-Yetholm as the locality in which it should make its first experiment. The details of the scheme were entrusted to Baird, upon whose recommendation the committee finally adopted the suggestion that, during the nine or ten months of the year the Gypsy parents were wandering throughout the land, their children should be kept at home and sent to school, or otherwise receive "temporal comfort and religious improvement". Also contained in the scheme were provisions for improving the schooling facilities. The parochial school at Town-Yetholm was in a deplorable condition : so, too, was the schoolhouse in Kirk-Yetholm. Baird himself described the latter building as "one of the most wretched hovels in which human beings were ever congregated". Through his efforts, a new and commodious school was erected in Kirk-Yetholm in 1843, and a suitable teacher installed.

The second and equally important part of the scheme proposed by Baird was calculated to induce this Gypsy population to abandon its idle and wandering existence, and to settle down to forms of regular employment. Over the more lawless of these vagabonds, he was able to exercise a greater influence than any of his predecessors. Yet, on one occasion, in the midst of his struggles for their salvation, they demonstrated their appreciation of him by invading his glebe and setting fire to his corn-stacks.

The death in 1859 of this excellent man, who deservedly won for himself the title of Saviour of the Gypsies, dealt a death-blow to the Society for the Reformation of the Gypsies. Almost immediately afterwards, this organization went to pieces. Since an integral part of the scheme was the education and care of the destitute and neglected children of the Gypsies, it has been said that Yetholm possessed the first Ragged School in Scotland.

\*    \*    \*    \*    \*

One summer's day in 1935, I arrived by car in this secluded

The Green o' Kirk-Yetholm at noontide in autumn, with Staerough in the background

A corner of the Green o' Kirk-Yetholm at 10 p.m. on Midsummer's Day

parish from Annan, after following devious Border byways. On the Green o' Kirk-Yetholm I got into conversation with a man who, I soon discovered, was the occupant of the Gypsy Palace. Although to-day there are no *real* Gypsies in Yetholm, thousands of people travel yearly in cars and charabancs to this village, especially on Sundays, to see the Palace, and to glean what they can of its former inhabitants. I inveigled my informant into becoming agreeably communicative on matters relating to this ancient Gypsydom. " I wes there masel' at the croonin' o' Chairlie Blythe, the Auld King ", this occupant of the royal apartment assured me. " That wes in 1898—thirty-seeven year ago. Thoosans and tens o' thoosans there, ye ken! The King had a kind o' plaitform put up for him. Then they put him on a chair ; and the chair was pu'ed by—och! ten donkeys wadna pu' the chair he wes on. It was that heavy. He had a croon on his heid. But, my! He wes an auld blaigard! He had awfie black een, jist terrible black they wes. His mither, ye ken, wes Queen Esther—Esther Faa Blythe, like. Ye'll hae heard o' her, nae doot. The folk that cam' tae see the King wes fair terrible—toffs an' the like. And, o' coorse, Esther Faa died, ye see. Then, fifteen year efter, they crooned Chairlie Blythe. The Queen, ye ken, reigned ower the Gypsies a lang, lang time. Ye'll hae heard tell o' her lang reign. She had great power ower her people. The Kingdom went tae bits efter Chairlie's death.

"Weel, A'm gang awa' hame tae the Palace for ma dennar !" he concluded with comical gesture, leaving me, fascinated, by the edge of the village Green.

All this helped me to find my bearings. With my eye, I followed him to his threshold, so that, a little later, I might visit the Gypsy Palace without having to make further enquiry as to where it was situated. I was to learn afterwards that Bob Taylor, with whom I had just parted company, was himself a potential claimant to the Gypsy throne!

I then noticed an intelligent-looking resident seated outside the most substantial house facing the Green o' Kirk-Yetholm. " Is there a cavern up there ?" I asked him, by way of inaugurating conversation, pointing meantime to a large, rectangular hollow in Staerough's cliffy face.

"No !" he replied affably. " It's no' a cavern. It's a cleft somewhat deceptive to the eye at this distance. We ca' it the Holly House here in Yetholm. When bairns are born in the district, and their elder brothers and sisters enquire too closely where they came from, it is customary for their parents to tell them, instead of the usual Santa Claus version of their origin, that the addition to the family came from the Holly House."

After the exchange of further observations pertinent to the locality, I came to learn that my informant was a man of some prominence and property. His name, as he now told me, was Robert Christie. Seldom have I met anyone quite so like a character lifted straight out of the pages of Walter Scott, and dropped down, quite appropriately, in the heart of the Borderland. His marriage to the owner of a good deal of property, both in Kirk-Yetholm and in Town-Yetholm, had earned for him the popular title of the Laird. His wife, a neat and couthie creature, hearing at the open window her ' man' in long and earnest conversation with a stranger, came to her threshold to invite me to come in and have tea. I accepted an invitation which gave me an opportunity of learning about the Gypsies from people who had known many of them, who were conversant with their history and lore, and who could enumerate all the crimes and petty delinquencies committed by them from the time of their settling in this neighbourhood, centuries ago. In this wise, incidentally, began one of the most cherished of my friendships.

" The Romany ways are here yet wi' them ", the Laird remarked, in referring to his neighbours. "Esther was Queen among them, as you've probably heard. She told fortunes; and she was a grand liar. A vindictive, auld hussy !

" But, man ! you should ha'e seen the Green there, when we had a waddin [wedding] or a funeral !" he continued. "It was something fair awful ! For local sprees and the like, Yetholm could beat any parish in Scotland, or in England, for that matter. Even though, I'd rather attend a Morebattle funeral than a Yetholm waddin." (Morebattle, by the way, is a neighbouring village famed, it is said, for the roisterous conduct associated with its burials, at which liquor flowed abundantly, according to custom.) From the Laird's description of ongoings at Yetholm, Border funerals and marriages were obviously occasions for excesses similar to those still prevalent in parts of the Highlands and Hebrides in connection with the *reitach*, or espousals, and with wakes and funerals. Visit almost any country churchyard in the Highlands and Islands with observant eye, and you are pretty certain to see a number of whisky bottles, eloquent as they are empty, in or about the dyke enclosing it, or thrown down among the long grass growing in the interior of any old ecclesiastical ruin within that churchyard!

" Tell me something about the last Gypsy coronation ", I now interposed.

" I will *that* ", replied the Laird. " There were ten thoosand folk here the day Chairlie Blythe was crooned, and twa hundred cuddies. He was crooned oot there on the Green o' Kirk-Yetholm ", he added, meanwhile moving the window-curtain aside, that I might see the very spot from his own ingle-neuk. " The Gypsies wended their way up the Loanings toward the tract o' land known as the Common. There they put a tin croon on him, and broke a bottle o' whisky ower his heid, and then bound a hare roond his neck. Chairlie then walked down the Loanings to his Palace as 'His Majesty!' The hare, of course, was indicative o' the chase—or, rather, o' the ancient art o' poaching, whereby the Gypsies derived so much o' their sustenance. They regarded poaching as their birthright, so to speak."

At this juncture my hostess took over the theme by recalling the doings of such Yetholm Gypsies as she herself had known. There was Rob, the Horner (he was a spoon-maker); Matthew, the Piper; Dave, the Fiddler; Auld Jake, the Fiddler's father; Stovie Jock; Jimmie, the Finisher (so called because he was the local grave-digger); Blythe, the Beadle, and grandfather of the present heir to the Gypsy throne; and so on. Among the quaint bynames at present recognized at Yetholm are Croxy, Braxy, Tottle the Bing, Auld Kruger, Bubbly Andrew, and Toddlie-up-the-road.

For my further edification, husband and wife then recited much of the Romany vocabulary of the district. Crab-apples, they told me, were called scrogs. In autumn, down by the haughs through which the Bowmont Water flows, one can gather scrogs by the bushel. Here, together with English equivalents, are some of the Gypsy words still in use at Yetholm:

| ROMANY | ENGLISH | ROMANY | ENGLISH |
|---|---|---|---|
| *Barrie glin* | a nice, cheery glow, as of a fire | Mas | flesh |
| | | Matchkin | cat |
| Bing | The De'il Himsel' | Neddies | potatoes |
| Blackies | pots and pans | Pani | water |
| Cadgie | a man | Peevan keir | public-house |
| Californie | chloroform | Peeve | to drink |
| Casties | sticks | Pig | hot water-bottle |
| Catchie | a policeman | Poke | bag |
| Chapin | mill | Rani | lady |
| Charry | baby | Ranking | enjoying |
| Chovy | shop | Shan | bad, evil |
| Cluach | stone | Shavies | bairns |
| Coories | blankets | Shero | head |
| Jigger | door | Tenty | careful |
| Kam | sun | Tod | fox |
| Kanné | hen | Winkler | window |
| Keir | house | Yag | fire, coal |
| Manishee | woman | | |

Later in the day the Laird escorted me over to the kirk. Engaged at odd jobs in the kirkyard at the time was John Blythe, the beadle at Kirk-Yetholm, and direct descendant of the royal family of Gypsydom. "The last Chairlie that wes crooned is in there", the beadle remarked, pointing to a strip of grassy ground near a juniper bush. Standing a few feet away was the headstone erected by Esther Faa and Charles Blythe in memory of their children who died in infancy. "Bar the psalm on the back-side o't", the beadle commented, "that's a' I can tell ye."

As we stepped inside the kirk, the beautiful chimes of the clock in the kirk-tower resounded through the sunlit valleys of the Cheviots, now waist-deep in ripening harvest. A wooden panel at the back of the kirk bears the names of all the ministers of Yetholm since the time of the Reformation—eighteen in all, commencing with the year, 1579, and including the present incumbent, the Rev. Kenneth MacFadden, M.A., who was inducted in 1925. In recent years, under Mr. MacFadden's influence, the interior of the kirk has been renovated most tastefully. The kirk is artistic and restful. Its stained-glass windows, donated by Andrew Blythe, cousin of the beadle, lend to it an air of quietude and mellowness—a mellowness strangely appropriate when the surrounding countryside stands deep in ripened grain.

Then I returned with the Laird to the historic Green o' Kirk-Yetholm—historic, I say, because it is steeped in Border history and in old-time Gypsy associations. Here, in point of brawling and fighting at any rate, were settled or accentuated all the Gypsies' age-long disputes: here rival claimants to the Gypsy throne fought pitched battles. Here, moreover, the celebrated Yetholm Herds Show was instituted more than a hundred years ago. Up to the outbreak of war in 1939, this event, held latterly at the Haugh of Town-Yetholm, was one of the few of any importance in the annals of this unsophisticated community, and of the hill-men dwelling remotely among the Border fells.

The main highway passing through this countryside divides the Green into two portions, approximately equal in area. On taking leave of the Laird and his wife on their doorstep by the fringe of it, and seeking the direction for Kelso and the highroad to Edinburgh, one was conscious of quitting the remnant of an age now passed—conscious, too, that one would have to return some day, to linger with notebook and camera.

At the time of the Teuchat Storm, or Peesweeps' Blast, as the folks of Ettrick and Teviotdale term the erratic snows falling in March and April, at lambing-time (since they are associated in these parts with the arrival of the green plover) I did return to Yetholm, after a hazardous journey over Soutra, the most westerly ridge of the Lammermuirs. There the Teuchat Snows lay so deep that, for several days, the king's highway between the Scottish Capital and England was impassable, and great stretches of the Borderland were isolated completely. Staerough wore a mantle of white; and a thin mist, the hue of birch catkins, veiled Yetholm's villages. For a moment or two, I halted by the old white Manse, situated among trees, and standing on a slight eminence just where one enters Kirk-Yetholm from Town-Yetholm. Sprinkled among the snows surrounding the Manse were snowdrops in greater profusion than I have seen them anywhere else in my life—characteristic, indeed, of the Borderland at the time of the Peesweeps' Blast. (Who has not heard of the snowdrops at Springwood, in the time of its poet-proprietor, the late Sir George Douglas?)

In course of conversation with an old woman I met near at hand, I learnt that the Rev. John Baird, who did so much to reclaim the Gypsies from their waywardness, was a great lover of flowers, and that, almost a century ago, the parishioners' children, under his direction, planted the precincts of the Manse with snowdrops. My informant added, and with a sense of pride, that, among those children, was her own mother. In gazing upon these tiny, storied harbingers of an earth awakening, I found myself unconsciously lilting a phrase of Frances Allitsen's music to that line from William Watson's *Lute Player*:

*In time of snowdrop, they were wed.*

I have often returned to Kirk-Yetholm to stay with the Christies, since that Teuchat Storm. A share in their hearth and board, and a warm, downy bed into which I can sink after a day's wandering among the Cheviots, have been vouchsafed to me ever since my first visit—ever since the day I found Robert Christie seated outside his house by the Village Green. Throughout the intervening years, he and I have remained in constant correspondence on one theme or another. He keeps me well posted in all the ongoings of the Borderland. I shall have to tell you more about these kindly folk.[1]

[1] See Dedication, pp. v-viii.

# CHAPTER FIVE

## WHO SHOT THE RED FOX?

" . . . Executed on this spot, Nov., 8th, 1752, for a crime of which he was not guilty."

With these dramatic words concludes the inscription on the granite monument commemorating James Stewart of Acharn, or James of the Glen, erected in 1911 by the Stewart Society on a knoll overlooking the narrows of Loch Leven and the Ballachulish Ferry, in Argyll. The monument, tradition maintains, actually stands over the holes into which the gibbet-posts had been placed. It is roughly eleven feet in height, and is crowned by a stone of white quartz of an irregular spherical shape, about two and a half feet in diameter, resting on a columnar pedestal.

And what crime is James alleged to have committed?

He was charged, after a fashion unique in the criminal annals of Scotland, with having been accessory to the murder of Colin Campbell of Glenure, factor for the forfeited estates of Ardsheal and Mamore, and commonly spoken of in the Highlands, even at the present day, as the Red Fox.

The arraignment of James Stewart before a packed jury at Inveraray for his alleged complicity in what since has been styled the Appin Murder, and his subsequent fate on Cnap Chaolais, the Gallows Hill, at Ballachulish, caused profound misgivings and forebodings throughout Scotland at the time. Persons known to have been out of favour with Archibald, third Duke of Argyll, now began to wonder when the Crown authorities, dominated by a Duke who, though holding the high office of Lord Justice-General of Scotland, was actuated by clan hatreds and rivalries rather than by conscience and a desire to administer the law with equity, might not likewise have them sentenced to death for crimes of which they were innocent.

Though nigh two centuries have elapsed since the Red Fox, mortally wounded, fell from his horse in the woods by the Appin shore, and since a guiltless man went to the gibbet to assuage the bloodthirstiness of the MacCailein Mòr and his Campbell Clan, traditions of the actual murder, and of the shameless departure from justice it occasioned, are still related in Appin and the impinging country with a familiarity similar to that one finds in Moidart and the Outer Hebrides, where, to this day, the country folks converse with one of Prince Charlie as though they had known him intimately, and had succoured him in his adversity. In Appin and elsewhere in Argyll I have met people who speak of James of the Glen as though they had been neighbours of his. With pride they remind one of the clan secret handed down from generation to generation to no more than one or two persons— that secret so jealously guarded, concealing from mankind the identity of the man who actually fired the shot which brought down the Red Fox.

*All are agreed that, whoever fired that shot, it was not James.*

For the world-wide fame this story has achieved, we are indebted to that incomparable artist, Robert Louis Stevenson. The death of Colin Campbell of Glenure, and the trial and subsequent condemnation of James Stewart, form the historical basis of *Kidnapped*, and of its sequel, *Catriona*—two of the most charming narratives in British fiction. The hardships and adventures of David Balfour, as set out so gracefully in the pages of *Kidnapped*, gave to the Appin Murder a prominence it has maintained, and to James an immortality of which he never dreamed. By 1886, the year in which *Kidnapped* was published, remembrance of James, and of the circumstances that found him condemned as an assassin, lingered only in the hearts of Highland folks with Jacobite sympathies—folks whose grandparents, in the bad, old days, had seen James's corpse dangling from the gibbet, and at a later date, after his bones had been picked clean by raven and carrion-crow, had witnessed the gruesome spectacle of his skeleton, re-wired more than once, as a warning to all who passed by.

Thanks largely to Stevenson, then, there are few episodes in the arduous history of Scotland so widely known as that notorious interference with the course of justice, culminating in the judicial murder in 1752 of a man against whom there was not a tittle of legitimate evidence, and of whose innocence the entire countryside was convinced. English-speaking people the world over, who have read Stevenson on the subject, and possibly also

Andrew Lang, still ask themselves the question, 'Who shot the
Red Fox?'

★　　★　　★　　★　　★

Situated in Duror of Appin is the farm of Acharn, tenanted in
1752 by James Stewart.  Prior to his coming to Acharn the
previous year, James had lived farther up Glen Duror.  In order
to distinguish him from others of his name, he became known
throughout the Stewart province of Appin as *Seumas a' Ghlinne*,
James of the Glen.  As the natural son of Ardsheal, the Stewart
chieftain to whom clansmen dwelling hereabouts owed allegiance,
he was deemed a man of some standing.  After 'The Forty-five'
his half-brother, who by this time had succeeded his father as
chieftain, went into exile.  Thus James, for the time being, became recognized leader of the Stewarts swearing fealty to Ardsheal.  In this capacity he commanded some measure of respect,
and acquired a moderate degree of authority.

For their espousal of the Jacobite cause, the Appin Stewarts
already had suffered heavily.  They had sacrificed themselves for
the Old Chevalier at Sheriffmuir; and nearly a hundred of them
had fallen at Culloden.  The lands of Ardsheal had been declared
forfeit; and their clans-people were now compelled to pay rents
to a Government that, virtually, had disinherited them, and had
attainted the chieftain, whom they revered.  In resisting the dis-
placement of the old dynasty in favour of the House of Hanover,
James of the Glen had played a prominent part.  When he took
up residence at Acharn with his wife and family, he was a man in
the full vigour of life, with the advantages over his oppressed
kinsmen of being able to read and write tolerably well, and of
possessing some practical knowledge of affairs.  He was, therefore, a person whose opinion was sought and respected.

In addition to his having reared three children of his own, James
undertook the care and upbringing of some children who had
been orphaned by the death of their father, a close kinsman of his.
One of these children was Allan Breac Stewart, who, in later life,
had his full share of adventure and der-doing.  Because of the
marks left upon him by smallpox, he received the appropriate
name of *Breac*, meaning speckled, or pock-marked.  His career
was a chequered one.  In early manhood he had been notorious

89

for his insobriety and reckless behaviour. He joined the Hanoverian forces, and was captured by the Jacobites at Prestonpans, whereafter he immediately enlisted in the cause of Prince Charlie. After Culloden he suffered outlawry, and escaped to France with many others who had staked their all on that grim and unfortunate enterprise. A life of inactivity in France did not appeal to Allan; and so he promptly enlisted in Ogilvie's Regiment, one of the three Scots regiments in the service of the French monarch. Soon he was promoted to officer rank. From time to time thereafter he paid visits to Appin, where, in addition to his interesting other men of military age in soldiering abroad, he collected from the natives such monies and gifts as they desired him to convey to Ardsheal, their exiled chief.

*　　*　　*　　*　　*

The spring of 1752 found Allan Breac on a visit to Appin and Mamore, where he had several relatives. He moved about the country freely, indifferent, it would seem, to his outlawry, fishing the pools and burns of Argyll with complete equanimity—indifferent also to the fact that his gaudy French apparel rendered him unduly conspicuous, and liable to seizure. A contemporary document describes him as a man of five feet ten inches in height, his face much marked with the smallpox, his black, bushy hair put up in a bag, slightly in-kneed, round-shouldered, black-eyed, about thirty years of age, "dressed much like a French cadet, shabby, with an inclination to be genteel".

No man in all Scotland or furth of her had a greater antipathy toward the Campbells than Allan; and, if there existed a member of that clan whom he detested more than another, that member was the Red Fox, Colin Campbell of Glenure. To the position of factor for the forfeited estates already mentioned, Glenure had been appointed in 1749; and it was only natural that, acting in this capacity, he should have occasioned the opprobrium of those Stewarts who resented that a Hanoverian Government was collecting, through him, rents they so willingly would have paid to the exiled Ardsheal. For a while matters appeared to be adjusting themselves: to all intents and purposes, the Appin folks were settling down under the new régime. Yet, underneath all this was a deep, secret loyalty to *Tearlach Og*—to Young Charlie

—and to those who had suffered with him, and also a corresponding desire to obstruct and undermine all who had usurped the authority of their rightful King.

This was the state of affairs Allan's visit accentuated in no small degree. High feelings soon came to high words; and high words eventually found expression in high-handed action. Coincident with Allan's sojourn in the Stewart country were the measures adopted by Glenure to evict from their farms certain tenants known to have Jacobite leanings, and suspected of transmitting to France, through the agency of Allan, monies that, on behalf of the Commissioners for the Forfeited Estates, Glenure fain would have claimed as escheat. Incensed by the fidelity of the Ardsheal people, the Hanoverian authorities now decided on removing them from the land, and entrusted Glenure with the task of putting into effect several notices to quit. The summer of 1751 witnessed James of the Glen evicted from his farm; and the spring of the following year found Glenure officially instructed to remove several other Ardsheal tenants by May, 15th—Whit Sunday—solely on the ground that they bore the names of clans with Jacobite sympathies, and were alleged to be disaffected toward the new order of things.

Against this arbitrary procedure there was no one more active than James Stewart. In espousing the cause of his dispossessed clansmen, he now found himself in deadly conflict with Glenure. In an endeavour to save the former, or at least mitigate the hardships to which they were to be subjected, he set out on a five days' journey to Edinburgh, where he hoped to procure a legal sist, or suspension of the evictions. But, though he tarried eleven days in the Capital, zealously pleading the cause of his kinsmen, his application finally was rejected on the representations of Glenure. He left Edinburgh on April, 19th, and arrived home in Appin on the 27th. On May, 5th, the day the court refused the suspension, a sheriff-officer was directed to evict several Stewart families from their ancient patrimony. The law now took its cruel, unrelenting course.

\* \* \* \* \*

A week or so later—on the day preceding the Whit Sunday term, to be precise—Colin Campbell of Glenure, in pursuance of his duties as factor, left Maryburgh (Fort William) for Appin, in company with John MacKenzie, his servant, Donald Kennedy, sheriff-officer at Inveraray, and Mungo Campbell, an Edinburgh 'writer', natural son of Campbell of Barcaldine, Glenure's brother. The party passed through Mamore, and crossed Loch Leven to Appin at the Ballachulish Ferry about five, intending to travel as far as Kentallen that evening, and to put the eviction orders into execution the following day. According to Mungo Campbell, who, as we have seen, was Glenure's natural nephew, and who eventually succeeded his murdered kinsman as factor for the Ardsheal estate, they carried between them " not a nail of arms ".

Along the hill-track still winding between Ballachulish and Kentallen they proceeded in Indian file. On reaching the Lettermore, a shot was fired by *someone*, and Glenure fell from his horse, mortally wounded. In a short space of time he was dead. Meanwhile, the figure of a man wearing a short, dark-coloured cloak, and carrying a gun, vanished in the thick coppice, and was observed, later, fleeing along the hillside. Whoever this man was, he made good his escape, and, in so doing, did much to bequeath to us the mystery that to this day, in the Highlands and elsewhere, prompts the question, *Who killed Colin Campbell of Glenure, the Red Fox?*

MacKenzie now rode ahead in search of assistance, leaving Mungo Campbell with the corpse, which eventually was conveyed from the Lettermore to a local inn. When, in the course of time, he chanced to pass by the farm of Acharn, he found James of the Glen there, quietly working in a field. He informed him of what had occurred. James immediately showed uneasiness, since he well understood what this tragedy involved for him and his kinsfolk. We are told that he " wrung his hands, and expressed great concern at what had happened, as what might bring innocent people to trouble ". He realized that, whoever fired the fatal shot, *he* would be blamed for it, and given very little opportunity of proving his innocence. He had not forgotten that, on more than one occasion, he had come into conflict with the Government's representatives in Argyll, either when challenging their authority directly, or when mediating on behalf of his harassed clansfolk. Moreover, he was aware that, when visiting the local change-houses, and not altogether fully in possession of his faculties, he sometimes had made indiscreet remarks of a braggart nature. Yet, he was sensible enough to recognize that to shoot, or to be accessory to the shooting of, the Forfeited Estates Commissioners' agent would have been sheer lunacy, if viewed but from the standpoint of his own personal safety.

\* \* \* \* \*

Anyhow, the heather was now afire. In Appin, a region essentially Jacobite in more than mere sympathy, one of the King's officers—and a member of the Clan Campbell at that!— had been assassinated. The old hatred and fury that Culloden had left smouldering in men's hearts were fanned into glowing flame. The Highlands were agog once more; and the rival factions they still harboured faced each other with renewed bitterness. In the Scottish Capital men in high authority now set themselves the task of devising means whereby *someone* could be found upon whom the blame for this tragedy, in part at all events, might be fixed, and in such a manner as to ensure that the Crown's representatives in future would be protected, and, if necessary, avenged.

As was only natural, suspicion fell on Allan Breac, who by now had sought timely refuge among the hills of Mamore and Glen Coe, which he knew so well, and who, before long, was back in France. In no time, more than a dozen persons were under arrest at Fort William, including James of the Glen and his sons. The entire countryside was now subjected to the closest investigation. James's home was ransacked for documentary evidence of his alleged complicity, while his wife and family were examined by methods that, nowadays, we would regard as Gestapo. Likewise with their neighbours. They, also, were bullied and threatened. Anyone who even dared suggest James's innocence was liable to immediate arrest and imprisonment on suspicion. All Appin was in a state of intimidation.

Meanwhile James lingered in confinement, access to direct and competent legal advice denied him. Even his wife was refused permission to visit him in prison. For this close isolation there was a reason. Strong as was the Campbell influence in matters affecting the judiciary, no risk could have been taken that might

93

have resulted in James's being tried by an impartial jury at Edinburgh, instead of at Inveraray, seat of the Duke of Argyll. Had the prisoner been allowed the advice to which he undoubtedly was entitled, he would have been on trial at Edinburgh within sixty days. There, in all probability, he would have been acquitted. The Argyll Circuit, on the other hand, was not due at Inveraray until September! Denial of adequate legal assistance, therefore, and corresponding delay, were to the Duke's advantage, if he were determined to secure James's conviction, irrespective of whether he was guilty or not. The Duke could rely on a jury composed chiefly of his own clansmen, assembled under his own presidency at Inveraray, to return a verdict that he well knew would not have been obtainable elsewhere in Scotland.

On August, 21st, Allan Breac and James Stewart were charged with having been "actors, or art and part" of the murder of Colin Campbell of Glenure. In a lengthy indictment prepared at the instance of the Lord Advocate, Allan was charged as principal, and James as accessory.

Thursday, September, 21st, 1752, was fixed as the date for James's trial. This was roughly four months after his arrest. Under armed escort, he was transferred to Inveraray from his detention at Fort William. For the first time, and by a piece of luck, he met, at Tyndrum, Mr. Stewart of Edinburgh, his agent. A consultation, necessarily brief and in the worst possible circumstances, took place there, as a result of which Mr. Stewart immediately hurried to Acharn to go through such of his client's papers as the Crown authorities had not already removed or destroyed. But it was not until three days before the prisoner stood his trial that, at Inveraray, he was given any reasonable opportunity of conferring with counsel. He was now more than fifty miles removed from the place where lived most of those who could have witnessed in his favour—a goodly step in a country as inaccessible as was Appin in the middle of the eighteenth century!

*　　*　　*　　*　　*

In the old court-house of Inveraray, and on the day appointed, the trial of the unfortunate James Stewart was opened. On the bench sat three judges—Lords Elchies and Kilkerran, and Archibald, third Duke of Argyll, Scotland's Lord Justice-General. The first two had had some considerable legal experience; and it is thought (as, indeed, it was thought at the time) that, had the trial been in *their* hands, and they had been free from influence or pressure on the part of the Duke, the prisoner might have received that measure of justice which the presidency of Argyll denied him throughout. At that time a candidate for the office of Lord Justice-General did not require to have any serious legal qualifications, with the result that it was often bestowed upon members of the Scottish nobility who were ludicrously lacking both in legal knowledge and acumen, and in a sense of justice and fairplay. Argyll's participating in this trial at Inveraray was quite contrary to precedent, by which the law frequently sets so much store. This is the only occasion, I believe, on which a Lord Justice-General has tried a case on circuit. In those days he seldom tried cases at all, even in Edinburgh. But, where the trial of James of the Glen was concerned, Argyll was primarily a Campbell, anxious to serve Campbell ends in a hereditary quarrel of long standing. Also contrary to precedent was the appearance on circuit at Inveraray of William Grant of Prestongrange, Lord Advocate, the Crown's chief adviser in Scotland on matters criminal.

Crown counsel also included James Erskine, Sheriff of Perth; Robert Campbell of Ashnish, well known as one of Argyll's many puppets; John Campbell of Levenside (afterwards Lord Stonefield); and Simon Fraser, son of Lovat of 'The Forty-five'. Fraser had been 'out' with Prince Charlie, and had commanded a contingent of his own clansmen in the Jacobite cause. Eventually he received a pardon from the Hanoverians, was called to the Scottish bar, and subsequently derived a good income by assisting his former enemies in circumventing his former allies.

Counsel for the prisoner were George Brown, Sheriff of Forfar; Thomas Miller, Sheriff of Kirkcudbright (who afterwards became, in succession, Solicitor-General, Lord Advocate, Lord Justice-Clerk, and Lord President of the Court of Session); Robert MacKintosh; and a young advocate named Walter Stewart.

The proceedings commenced with an attempt by the prisoner's counsel to have his client acquitted by what is known as a plea in bar of trial. Stewart argued that, since the prisoner was accused of being an *accessory*, it was improper to proceed against him so long as the *principal* was in doubt, and certainly at large. In short, his contention was that, until Allan Breac could also be put on trial, it was manifestly unfair to try James. The plea in bar was summarily dismissed by the court, and reasonably so, we think.

On the following day the jury was empanelled. And this is where Argyll so flagrantly abused his power. As presiding judge, he was at liberty to choose the sort of jury he liked, without any restriction whatsoever. Jurymen in those days were often selected in this way, in order to obtain conviction or acquittal. In any case, at the instance of Argyll, Lord Justice-General of Scotland, thirty-four eligible jurors were cited. Out of the total of fifteen finally empanelled, no fewer than eleven were Campbells. The remaining four comprised a MacNeil, a MacDougall, a Duncanson, and a Gillespie. Among those cited were at least three Stewarts, not one of whom was chosen. Eleven of the possible jurors hailed from Bute: not one of them was chosen either. Argyll now had a jury packed with his own clansmen, as was necessary to ensure the verdict for which he had schemed so ruthlessly. As the verdict in Scotland goes by majority, he certainly had the majority he required. It is doubtful whether, in all the criminal annals of this country, a jury has been empanelled quite so deliberately and blatantly, with a view to securing conviction irrespective of evidence. Certainly, there have been few juries of whose members it might be said with greater truth that they acted with malice aforethought.[1]

\*     \*     \*     \*     \*

It was important, of course, for the prosecution to be able to attach to Allan Breac primary responsibility for the murder of

[1] Contemporary documents would seem to disclose that the jury which tried James Stewart was not more Campbell in its constituents than was usual at Inveraray at this time. Generally speaking, a Campbell majority was to have been expected. If one take the County of Argyll as a whole, it seems that any jury empanelled from the ranks of the landed proprietors and tacksmen would have contained a high percentage of Campbells, especially when we remember that all parties known to have been active in the Jacobite interest, or even faintly in sympathy with it, were carefully excluded. This does not dispose of the contention that the jury concerned was a packed one. It shows, on the contrary, that, where matters of high political feeling were involved, the majority of the jury was bound to be prejudiced, and the verdict predictable before the trial opened.

Loch Linnhe and the Mountains of Ardgour from the Ballachulish Ferry

Tablet in the wall of the old, ruined church of Keil, in Appin.
" Here lie the remains of
JAMES STEWART
'Seumas a' Ghlinne'
who died 8th November, 1752"

Glenure. Otherwise it would have been difficult to convict James on the ground of his having been accessory. Briefly stated, the evidence against Allan might be summarized as follows:

1. A witness named Robert Stewart stated that he had heard Allan, when the worse of drink, say that, before he quitted Scotland again, he would dispose of Glenure.

2. Malcolm MacColl, the innkeeper at Portnacroish, in Appin, deponed that on one occasion Allan, when standing him a dram, remarked that he would give him something much better, if he succeeded in bringing to him the Red Fox's pelt. Aware that Colin Campbell was nicknamed the Red Fox, or Red Colin, this witness admitted that, on reflection, Allan's statement suggested a bribe to encompass Glenure.

3. Archibald MacInnes, the Ballachulish ferryman, averred that, on the day of the murder, Allan Breac had come to enquire of him whether Glenure had crossed the ferry.

4. The witness, Angus MacDonald, swore that Allan had told him of his detestation of the Clan Campbell, and that this detestation had been accentuated by Glenure's having informed the commandant at Fort William of his (Allan's) presence in the vicinity, and of his having suggested his apprehending him as a deserter.

5. The witness, Duncan Campbell, corroborated Angus MacDonald's evidence, adding that Allan had told him to inform his friends of the fate that would befall Glenure and his subordinates, if they evicted the Ardsheal tenants. Indeed, Duncan Campbell went further, in that he deponed to Allan's having said that, if he should encounter Glenure under suitable conditions, he would get even with him.

Taking it all in all, it cannot be said that this evidence amounted to much. Whereas there may have been substantial ground for the view that Allan Breac may have known beforehand of the proposed murder, there was not produced a tittle of evidence to support the contention that it was *he* who fired the shot. His attitude toward Glenure, and indeed toward the whole Campbell

G

Clan, was common knowledge. But so was the attitude of hundreds of others in Argyll and elsewhere in Scotland. At various times, doubtless, many ardent Jacobites in Appin had expressed all manner of malice against the Campbells, and even bragged of what they intended doing to Glenure. In those days of clan strife, abuse of prominent members of another clan was quite an ordinary feature of everyday life. Threats of violence, likewise, were the rule rather than the exception, though it is doubtful whether, even in those harsh times, more than the merest fraction of threats uttered was carried into execution. So far as this was concerned, therefore, the evidence of Allan Breac's guilt was no more substantial than that which might have been preferred against scores of persons with avowed anti-Hanoverian sympathies.

As for Allan's enquiry of MacInnes, the ferryman, it did not necessarily prove anything. The evictions to which Glenure was proceeding were no fresh departure. Numerous evictions had been carried through under his instructions; and the particular evictions then pending in Appin had already been given prominence in the courts at Edinburgh. At the time of the murder, everyone knew how imminent they were. Allan's query as to whether Glenure had crossed the ferry was quite an excusable one in the circumstances. It did not necessarily justify the deduction that he was lurking in the vicinity in the hope that a suitable opportunity would present itself when *he* might encompass the factor's life. The most one is entitled to assume from the ferryman's statement is that Allan knew something unlawful was afoot. Beyond his knowledge of this, it is difficult to establish any guilt.

Allan's flight immediately after the incident does not prove that he even had knowledge of any plan devised to rid the countryside of Glenure. Allan was a deserter, it must be remembered. He had been outlawed. No one in his position, anxious to retain his freedom, however innocent he might have been of the murder, was likely to linger in the locality, knowing that, in any case, suspicion was bound to rest heavily upon him.

Two further points in Allan's favour might be mentioned in passing. On the day of the tragedy, the gun he had been accustomed to was at Acharn. Allan at that time was moving among his friends elsewhere in Appin. So, if Allan fired the fatal bullets which, as the late David MacKay points out in his exhaustive treatise, were undeniably well aimed, he did so with an unfamiliar weapon, in days when marksmanship was a very inexact science.[1]

The second point adverts to Mungo Campbell, who, you will recall, was one of the company with Glenure when he dropped from his horse. Mungo observed the murderer's escape; and Allan Breac, a knock-kneed fellow, was known to Mungo. It seems strange that Mungo never made any suggestion that the fugitive he saw had anything peculiar about his gait!

*　　*　　*　　*　　*

Let us now examine the Crown's case against James.

Assuming that Allan actually fired the shot in the woods of the Lettermore, what evidence had the Lord Advocate that James was accessory? Here we find as weak a case in law as was the case against the fugitive Allan. Though a countryside, then white-hot with rival prejudices, was ransacked for evidence, and the Crown conducted the precognitions of hundreds of persons, the sum-total of the evidence it obtained against James Stewart amounted to little more than might have justified a reasonable suspicion of complicity, and, consequently, his temporary detention while investigations were being made.

From the historian's point of view, it is indeed unfortunate that, among the archives of the Court of Justiciary at Edinburgh, there is not preserved the official account of this engrossing trial. According to the records of the Barons of Exchequer, more than seven hundred precognitions were taken; and it is surely strange that no trace of these is to be found. It has been suggested, of course, that, as the trial was bound up with issues of major political import, special precautions were adopted to ensure the secret custody of such documentary matter. It is not altogether unlikely, then, that one day it may come to light.

When glancing through the inventory of the John MacGregor Collection, bequeathed to H.M. Register House, Edinburgh, by the late John MacGregor, W.S., in 1937, my eye fell upon item 166: "The Appin Murder—Letters, Declarations, Accounts, and

[1] *The Appin Murder*, p. 35.

other Documents relative to the prosecution of James Stewart of Acharn for the murder of Colin Campbell of Glenure, 1752. One original letter, remainder copies, 1 vol. 4to titled *The Appin Murder.*" In turning over this fascinating document, I found, among much else, an abstract of the precognitions reduced to general heads, and referring to the witnesses. Here is a selection from such as were designed to implicate both Allan and James:

"That Allan Breck Stewart was in great intimacy and familiarity with James Stewart and his family, and lived often at his house, which was his principal resort."

"That Allan Breck Stewart exprest strong resentment against Glenure and the Tenents to whom he had let James Stewart's farm, and threatened Glenure's Life on account of the removing of the other Tenents, and also for giving information against himself to have him put in custody."

"That about this time James Stewart and Allan Breck were particularly inquisitive about Glenure's motions."

"That on the 8th of May, Allan Breck with Charles Stewart, son of James, came to Stewart of Fasnacloich's house, which lyes opposite to Glenure's house (who was then expected from Edinburgh) where they were sure to learn Glenure's motions in going to Fort William. And that Allan was then drest in his own cloathes, being a long blew coat, red waistcoat, black breeches, and a feathered hat."

"That, after Glenure left his own house to go to Fort William on Monday the 11th of May, Allan Breck went directly to James Stewart's house, had some private conversation with James, changed his own cloathes, and put on a black short coat, Trewsars, and a blew Bonnet belonging to Jas. Stewart, who supt with Breck that night and saw him next morning."

"That on Tuesday morning Allan Breck went in James Stewart's Cloathes to Balachilishe's house & from that to Glenco's house, whose stepmother is a sister of Ardsheal's, and from that went to Collart's house, who is a nephew of James Stewart's, where he staid all night, and on Wednesday he came again to Glenco's, and from that went to Mr. Stewart of Ballachillishe's house, which lyes closs by the Ferry of Ballachilish that Glenure must pass in returning from Fort William, he staid there all Wednesdays night."

"That on Thursday about 12 o'clock Allan Breck went to fish upon a Burn that runs by Ballachilishe's house. That he fish't up the Burn into a woody place where he was in cover but as the ground rose gave him an opportunity of seeing the ferry and all the road that Glenure would take after he crost the ferry untill he entered the Wood of Lettermore where he was killed and from the place Breck was he had a very short cut to that Wood."

"That on the Sunday after the murder Allan Breck was seen lurking in the midst of a bush of wood at Coalisnacoon about a mile from the houses by Mary McDonald. That on her approache he started up with the appearance of apprehension. That he seemed to darn himself, and she suspected him then to be guilty of the murder."

"That James Stewart knew where Allan Break [sic] sculked after the murder. That he sent him money and his own cloaths. That Allan Break sculk'd in the Wood of Coolisnacoon untill he got the money and cloaths sent him by James Stewart. That after he got these he departed and has not been seen since."

★   ★   ★   ★   ★

Solely upon the following evidence, then, the Crown proceeded against James as alleged accessory:

1. He had come into open conflict with Glenure on the matter of the Appin evictions, and had striven hard to obtain a stay of execution.

2. His association with Allan Breac was long-standing, intimate, and undeniable.

3. Both he and Allan were known to have made indiscreet remarks about the same time on their attitude to Glenure in particular, and to the Campbells in general. In regard to the former, the witness, John Breac MacColl, swore that, a couple of years before the tragedy, he was present when James of the Glen said that he would "spend a shot upon Glenure, tho' he went upon his knees to his window to fire it".

4. This same witness declared that Allan, when seeking refuge after the murder, expressed the fear that the consequences might involve James and his elder son.

5. It was not denied that, on the day of Glenure's death, Allan was wearing a suit of clothes belonging to James.

6. There was proof that James, on hearing of Glenure's fate, exhibited some anxiety for his own personal safety. As mentioned earlier, he received the news from John MacKenzie with considerable alarm.

"Whoever the rider is, he is not riding his own horse!" said James, ominously, to a companion, on hearing a horseman approach.

"Glenure has been shot!" shouted MacKenzie, the horseman, on reaching the field in which James and his companion were working.

"Well", said James, "whoever did it, *I* am the man that will hang for it!"

7. There was evidence that after the murder, James and his wife had remitted money to Allan Breac.

Moreover, there were points in James's sworn declarations which were regarded as evidential. He admitted, for instance, that, shortly after the murder, several of the neighbouring tenants came to ask him what they should do, and whether they should go near the corpse, and that he advised them to do so, while he and Allan stayed away from it. This was looked upon as further proof of guilt. James's explanation for having absented himself was that he wished to avoid meeting Campbell of Ballieveolan and his sons, whom he knew would be there, and with whom he was scarcely on the best of terms, and for a reason he gives, namely, that "there were some chagrine betwixt him and them, they having taken the declarant's possession a year before".[1]

In addition to this, the jury had before it a certain amount of written evidence. Although even at the time the wife and children

---

[1] It has been suggested, however, that James's avoidance was dictated rather by his belief in the ancient superstition that the corpse of a murdered person will bleed in the presence of the murderer or of his accomplices. This explanation was given many years ago to Duncan C. MacTavish, Inveraray, and is referred to in that admirable selection from the Inveraray Papers published for him in booklet form by the *Oban Times* in 1939. That this belief was current in Argyllshire earlier in the same century is shown by the following extract from the report of the examination of Margaret Campbell before the kirk-session of Glassary, dated the 29th, March, 1705: "The Examination and Confession of Margaret Campbell alias Guinach who is suspected to have murthered her owne childe. . . . This day the said Margaret Campbell before she made the forsed confession, she being in the Church before the Min[r] and several Elders and manie other witnesses was desired to handle her dead childe befor it was putt in the coffine, which she doeing it was visible to severall that some red freshlike blood dropt from the childes head and face and from the corps upon the dale where it lay, and particularlie she being againe desired to handle the corps and she keeping her hand some little time upon the childes thigh where the skin was whole, after she removed her hand from off it there appeared about the breadth of a fourteen penie all read of a bloodie colour."

In the case of the Mures of Auchendrane (1611) suspicion was fixed upon them because they failed to compear when all the men of the district were summoned to touch the corpse of the murdered man. This suspicion was regarded as having been justified beyond question when the corpse bled at the approach of Mary Mure, "auld Auchendrane's" daughter.

According to Pitcairn, at the trial of James Howatson for murder, held at Dumfries in 1727 before Lord Justice-Clerk Cockburn, it was insisted that the accused's guilt was further shown by his refusal to go to the lifting of the corpse.

of an accused person could not be forced to give evidence either for or against him, the authorities in this case had conducted private examinations of James's wife and their three children. It was decided to utilize their signed depositions, compulsorily obtained, in the drawing up of the indictment, since they tended to reveal discrepancies such as might cast a doubt on the truthfulness of any witnesses for the defence. Had the bench not departed from the age-long practice in the Scottish courts, it would have rejected such evidence, and in so doing possibly castigated the Lord Advocate, as Crown prosecutor, for having desired to introduce it.

The importance of this evidence was emphasized by Simon Fraser, who had been instructed in the case because of his knowledge of the Gaelic, which was the only tongue properly understood by so many of the witnesses. Despite renewed protest by defending counsel against this irregularity, Argyll held that such evidence was competent, and his fellow-judges acquiesced.

*　　*　　*　　*　　*

All through that woeful Friday and Saturday, the trial of James of the Glen proceeded in the old court-house at Inveraray, without interruption. Late on Saturday evening the Lord Advocate addressed the jury on as flimsy a charge as the Crown in Scotland has ever preferred against a prisoner. Of the threat sworn to by John Breac MacColl, he made the most: there was, indeed, very little else to go upon; and even the evidence of this was far from satisfactory.

By daybreak the following morning, the jury found itself listening to Mr Brown's concluding speech on behalf of the prisoner. His task in ordinary circumstances would have been a simple one, for the court would readily have dismissed a case based upon evidence so inadequate, so trivial, and so obviously obtained under duress. But he had to contend against the overweening ambition of Argyll that James *must* be found guilty. To succeed in a court so biassed, and against jurymen known to have been selected for the sole purpose of perverting the course of justice, seemed hopeless from the start.

"The panel's guilt", continued Mr. Brown, "is still the more improbable as he could not possibly propose any benefit by it.

He was a man of too good understanding not to see that Glenure's place as factor would soon be supplied, that the strictest search would be made for the authors of this enormous crime, and that his family, as being nearly connected with the forfeited person, would be first suspected. Is it possible that in such circumstances it could enter into the imagination of the panel to commit a crime of so black a nature, when he could not only reap no benefit by it, but when it behoved necessarily to involve his own family in inevitable distress and ruin ?"

In the course of a long and thorough scrutiny of the evidence alleged against James, the jury was reminded that one witness deponed to having heard the notorious cateran, Sergeant Mòr Cameron, say he would put a bullet through Glenure when the opportunity presented itself. To a large extent, this evidence was corroborated.

"Pray, sir, cut it short!" interposed one of the Campbell jurors—Campbell of Southall. "We have had enough of it, and are quite tired, the trial having lasted long."

Though it now appeared more hopeless than ever, counsel for the defence continued.

If Argyll, as presiding judge, addressed the jury, as was the custom even then, there seems to be no record of it. If he did, he must have done so in the tersest terms. In any event, to have made any attempt to sum up was quite superfluous : the verdict already was foregone.

The trial (if by such a name it may be dignified!) had been in progress fifty hours when, about eight o'clock on Sunday morning, the jury retired to consider its verdict. Not even the strict observance of the Sabbath was allowed to intervene. "The better the day, the better the deed" runs the proverb. A Campbell had been murdered. None but a Stewart could have committed such a crime. And here, in Argyll's eyes, was the Stewart who would have to pay the penalty with his life. About four hours later, the jury unanimously returned a verdict of guilty ; and in due course a formal interlocutor was signed by Argyll, as presiding judge, and by Lords Elchies and Kilkerran, consigning the unfortunate James to his doom—condemning him "to be hanged by the neck upon a gibbet by the hands of an executioner until he be dead, and thereafter to be hung in chains upon the said gibbet".

Thus, Argyll won in a clan feud that had lasted so long, and had brought destruction to many an innocent victim. "If you had been successful in that rebellion", said Argyll, in addressing the condemned man, "you would have been now triumphant with your confederates, trampling upon the laws of your country, the liberties of your fellow-subjects, and on the Protestant religion. You might have been giving the law where you now have received the judgment of it, and we, who are this day your judges, might have been tried before one of your mock Courts of judicature, and then you might have been satiated with the blood of any name or clan to which you had an aversion."

It is recorded that, throughout this ordeal, James conducted himself with great restraint and composure. In acknowledging his submission to the sentence of death passed on him, he forgave the jury and the witnesses "who have sworn several things falsely against me, and I declare, before the great God and this auditory, that I had no previous knowledge of the murder of Colin Campbell of Glenure, and am as innocent of it as a babe unborn. I am not afraid to die, but what grieves me is my character, that after ages should think me capable of such a horrid and barbarous murder."

Thereafter he was removed to Fort William to await the day appointed for his execution. And it was written of him that, while languishing there, "he behaved in every respect so like a good Christian that his greatest enemies were forced to commend him".

★ ★ ★ ★ ★

On *Cnap Chaolais Mhic Pharuig*, the knoll situated but a stone's-throw from the hotel at South Ballachulish, James of the Glen, on November, 8th, 1752, hung from the gibbet "until he be dead." Two clergymen and a few intimate friends were with him in his last moments on earth. Before the end, he expressed a wish to have the 35th Psalm read to him. And to this very day the old folks of Appin and Lochaber refer in the Gaelic to this Psalm as *Salm Sheumais a' Ghlinne*, the Psalm of James of the Glen. A prayer was then put up for him; and he read a statement protesting his innocence. One copy of this statement he handed to the sheriff, who was present. Another he gave to the officer in charge of the soldiers deputed to take his life.

In strict accord with the letter and spirit of the sentence, and in order that it might be a warning to others, his body was duly hung in chains. For a long time it remained guarded, lest some of his Ardsheal kinsfolk should attempt to rescue it, and give it decent burial. The birds of prey haunting the Appin hills and the Loch Linnhe shores soon picked clean the bones, which, when they began to fall apart, were articulated with wires, so that James's skeleton might continue to provide a gruesome reminder to those still secretly in fealty to 'the King o'er the Water'. Three years or so later, it fell to the ground. Tradition has it that, by this time, Campbell spying had abated sufficiently to have enabled some Ardsheal Stewarts and their friends, clandestinely, to carry away, for reverent burial in the family mools at Keil, such of James's bones as were left when rough justice and the carrion-fowl had finished with them. The bones were actually removed by three brothers named Livingstone, one of whom was Neil, grandfather of David Livingstone. In the wall of the old, roofless kirk at Keil is a small, bronze tablet marking the spot where they ultimately committed to earth all that remained of James.

"Here lie the remains of

JAMES STEWART

'Seumas a' Ghlinne'

who died 8th November 1752"

\*   \*   \*   \*   \*

According to the Dewar MSS. at Inveraray, there were but three guns available in Appin and Nether Lochaber at the time of the fatality, owing to the stringency imposed by the Disarming Act. All three, at the material time, appear to have been requisitioned by the young bloods of the district, who were thought to have entered into conspiracy to remove Glenure by felony.

One of these guns—a long, Spanish one—belonged to Dugald MacColl, who named it *An t-Slinneanach*, The Broad-shouldered. By this title it became well known in the locality. "It was an excellent gun for casting bullets", we read. "Were a bullet and swan-shot put in it, it would cast the two within an inch of each other at the distance of one hundred yards." The same authority informs us that this gun was handed to Donald Mac-Donald Stewart, "brother-son [*i.e.*, nephew] to the Laird of Ballachulish; and Fasnacloich was to be with him to shoot Colin".

But there are several guns said to be the one that brought down Glenure—claimed to be the weapon known to the Gaels as *an gunna dubh a mhifhortain*, the Black Gun of Misfortune. One such is said to lie at the bottom of Loch Creran, in Appin.

Some years after the tragedy, a maidservant, Janet MacInnes by name, while tending cattle in Gleann a' Chaolais, the glen behind Ballachulish House, discovered a gun in the hollow of a large elder-tree. On taking it home with her, she showed it to "Old Mr. Stewart of Ballachulish", who instantly exclaimed, "'*Se sin an gunna dubh a mhi-fhortain, a Sheonaid!* That, Janet, is the Black Gun of Misfortune!" Mr. Stewart, incidentally, was almost the last man to have spoken to Glenure before he was shot.

This may have been the gun once owned by his nephew, Donald, aforementioned. If so, it might explain how it came to be found in the glen behind Ballachulish House.

*It is believed by many that Donald MacDonald Stewart fired the fatal shot.*

Why should Mr. Stewart have been so familiar with this gun as to have pronounced on it so spontaneously, so gravely? Had he seen it before? Did he recognize it as the weapon at some time used by, if not actually belonging to, his nephew? For several years it remained at Ballachulish House as an interesting, if somewhat gruesome, relic.

In 1938 there was deposited in the West Highland Museum, at Fort William, the exhibit labelled "Gun of Appin". This gun was once the property of the late Mrs. MacDonald Stewart of Dalness, in Glen Etive. It came to Fort William from Lord Antrim, at Dalness House, where it had reposed for some sixty years. When I made enquiries recently of Mr. MacAndrew, Curator of the West Highland Museum, he informed me, with some regret, that experts at the Royal Scottish Museum, at Edinburgh, to whom he had taken it for examination and comment, pronounced it to be an old Afghan gun, unknown in 1752, and therefore unlikely to have been the one used in the Appin Murder. In face of this authority, he felt he could do no more than describe it as labelled. Tradition has it, of course, that the Black Gun was of *Spanish* make.[1]

\* \* \* \* \*

In 1753 the incorrigible Sergeant Mòr was hanged for a murder he had committed at Braemar.

As for the elusive Allan Breac Stewart, he was alive in France during the French Revolution. Scott tells us, in a footnote to his introduction to *Rob Roy*, that, about 1789, at the dawn of the Revolution, a friend of his, then resident in Paris, was invited to witness, from the windows of an apartment occupied by a Scottish Benedictine priest, a procession which, it was thought, might be of interest to him. "He found, sitting by the fire, a tall, thin, raw-boned, grim-looking old man, with the *petit croix* of St. Louis. His visage was strongly marked by the irregular projections of the cheekbones and chin. His eyes were gray. His grizzled hair exhibited marks of having been red, and his complexion was weather-beaten, and remarkably freckled. Some civilities in French passed between the old man and my friend, in the course of which they talked of the streets and squares of Paris, till at length the old soldier, for such he seemed, and such he was, said with a sigh, in a sharp Highland accent, '*Deil ane o' them a' is worth the Hie Street o' Edinburgh!*'

"He was none other than the Freckled Allan—Allan Breac."

According to Scott, Allan was then living decently on his small pension, and had, by this time, divested himself of all traces of "the savage mood, in which he is generally believed to have assassinated the enemy and oppressor, as he supposed him, of his family and clan".

\* \* \* \* \*

Who, then, shot the Red Fox?

To this day in Appin, they say, there is handed down, traditionally, and in solemn secrecy, the name of the culprit. Robert Louis Stevenson failed to elicit from the Gaels of western Argyll the identification of "the other man", as he is still referred to in

[1] Apart from the gun, however, the West Highland Museum is replete with beautiful and historic things associated with 'The Fifteen' and 'The Forty-five'—a tribute to the zeal of the late Victor Hodgson, its founder and first curator, whose untimely passing, a few years ago, robbed Celtic Scotland of one of her most ardent enthusiasts.

the Highlands. Andrew Lang, who, with his penchant for exploring history's alluring byways, *claimed* to have probed this Celtic secret, mentions the tradition that, on the day of James's execution, "the other man" wanted to give himself up, and was prevented from doing so by kinsfolk and friends, no fewer than six of whom forcibly held him until the sentence pronounced at Inveraray had been carried out, urging that no confession would save James, and that, in all probability, the confessor would share a similar fate. The whole of the facts were known to several persons prior to the execution, according to Lang, who adds that "at least one of those persons had to be bound with ropes by his family to prevent his going to the scaffold on the fatal morning to make the facts known". In Lang's view (though he quotes no authority for it) this was the murderer. He informs us, further, that the house in which this incident occurred was still standing in Ballachulish at the time of his visit. Could it have been Ballachulish House, in at least one apartment of which were heard those strange noises and knockings to which Andrew Lang refers? And might the bound man not have been Donald Mac-Donald Stewart, nephew of Stewart of Ballachulish? The elder-tree, in which Janet found the gun, you may remember, grew in the valley just behind Ballachulish House!

It has never been disputed that several men, many of them Camerons from Appin and Lochaber, were concerned with Allan Breac in a scheme to bring down the Red Fox when an opportunity presented itself. Neither has it been questioned that many lay in wait for him the day he was shot. The man who was bound with ropes on the morning of the execution to prevent his reaching the Gallows Hill at South Ballachulish, there to confess his guilt, was one of these. There is good ground for believing that he was a young man of some importance, whose confession, both in the eyes of James and of those who restrained him, would merely have involved others in peril.

Andrew Lang not only failed to disclose the name of "the other man", but expressed his determination never to do so. For my own part, I do not think he ever knew! (Authors frequently are given to a touch of the melodramatic: they have an idea it impresses their readers.) He clearly believed that Sergeant Mòr Cameron was innocent of the murder; and, in any event, the sergeant was hanged in 1753, as already mentioned. There was no necessity, therefore, for secrecy so far as *he* was concerned. A few days after the murder, Allan was back in France, well out of the reach of Campbell justice. So the secret could not have been designed to shield *him*.

For all that, there was, and may still be, a hereditary secret, withholding that name from the common knowledge of men, and handed on from generation to generation at death-bed, in Appin.

Many years ago, when wandering through Argyll in search of material that ultimately formed the nucleus of my book, *Wild Drumalbain: The Road to Meggernie and Glen Coe*, I found myself in conversation at Onich with Hugh Cameron, the piermaster, one of the most perfervid of Jacobites. Hugh told me of an ancestor of his, who had been standard-bearer to Lochiel during 'The Forty-five'; and with solemnity he invited me into his small shed on the pier, that he might show me some cherished Jacobite relics he kept there. With discretion, I broached the matter of the secret, and soon learned from him that, in due course, *he* expected to be its hereditary custodian. His eyes sparkled as he told me of how the Appin folks had denied to the author of *Kidnapped* the name of him who shot the Red Fox, and had also left Andrew Lang with his conjectures. Waving his hand in an ominous manner toward the Appin shore, less than a mile away, he remarked in measured tones: "*There's an old man living over yonder, who knows the clan secret!*" From him, doubtless, Hugh Cameron expected to inherit it. For all we know, he may have done so, and passed it on to yet another custodian.

The pier at Onich is now grass-grown and decayed: the steamer no longer calls. When revisiting the pier in 1945, I had to walk warily on those planks over which, but a few years before, passengers could hurry with safety, even on the windiest of days. The shed in which Hugh kept his relics, as also the cabin-like structure, round the interior of which waiting passengers sat, and often shivered in wintry weather, is now quite forlorn, except for the curious few who, like myself, cannot pass by without pausing at a spot haunted by one from whom we might have wrested the clan secret, or for the collies from the neighbouring cottages, when they come to chase away the seagulls perched on the bollards at the end of the pier. What changes even a few years' desertion can wreak upon a scene once trod so gaily, so confidently, by the feet of men !

*     *     *     *     *

Much still remains of James Stewart's house at Acharn. In recent years it was roofed with corrugated iron, and is now used as part of the steading belonging to the farm of Acharn, situated in the lower reaches of Glen Duror of Appin.

At best, this dwelling, consisting of one floor and two small apartments, could have offered but humble accommodation to James, his wife, and their three children. Their two sons, as also Allan Breac when he resided with them, were obliged to sleep in the adjoining barn, not a stone of which now stands upon another.

Glenure House, of course, is still inhabited. The dressing-room off the Red Fox's bedroom—the apartment into which his body was carried—has a floor-board with a bloodstain denoting the spot where it lay. So carefully has this bloodstain been preserved that, when an acquaintance of mine visited the Stanhopes there in 1934, it was actually pointed out to him. I am told, also, that the floor of this same room shows the stain of blood which had dripped from the dead man's garments as they hung from a peg.

A letter I received recently from Ballachulish, written by that indefatigable historian, the late Hugh G. MacColl, then honorary treasurer of the Clan MacColl Society,[1] contains an interesting reference to this bloodstain. "When writing you in 1944 about the Appin Murder", he says, "I mentioned that I had seen a bloodstain in the room at Glenure where Colin Campbell was taken after he was killed, and I think you wondered how it was that the bloodstain was still there. I was speaking recently to Mr. Philip Spencer Stanhope, a brother of the late proprietor of Glenure, and uncle of Mrs. Spencer Stanhope, the present owner, and he confirmed that there *was* this room with the bloodstain. He explained that the room had been completely closed up for about a hundred years (presumably just as it was after the Red Fox was killed) and re-opened within com-

---

[1] He was killed at the age of 45 in a motor accident at Stirling in April, 1947, soon after these pages had gone to the printer.

paratively recent times. This probably accounts for the preservation of the bloodstain."

Miss MacKay, one of my many correspondents in the Highlands, writes me from Connel that, when her great-grandfather, John MacIntyre, took over Glenure House toward the end of the eighteenth century, the Red Fox's garments were still there. Eventually, they passed into the possession of Professor Campbell Fraser, whose grandmother was Glenure's sister, and whose son, recently deceased, wrote an excellent book on the Campbells of Barcaldine.[1]

On my receiving Mr. Hugh MacColl's letter, I wrote to Mr. Philip Spencer Stanhope, whom he mentions, asking him whether he could tell me anything about the bloodstain, or about the clothes the Red Fox was wearing when shot.

"I can give you the following account", he replied, "as told me by Mr. Peter MacKay, now resident in Sydney. The Campbells let Glenure as a farm to the MacKays.

"At the time of the murder of the Red Fox, there was at Glenure House a panelled room and a dressing-room attached to one another. Each had one window, with narrow panes of glass and heavy oak frames, as was the custom then against housebreakers, but giving very little light. After the murder, the body was brought into the dressing-room and stripped of its clothes. These were hung on a peg by the Campbells, who then locked the room up. During the lifetime of Mr. MacKay's grandfather, that room was never entered. When his father renovated the windows throughout the house, putting plate glass in them, the window of the dressing-room was not touched. This room, because it remained locked and was never entered, and because its window, as seen from the outside, looked peculiar, became known as the Haunted Room.

"However, Mr. Peter MacKay, after his father's death, prized open the door, and there he saw Colin Campbell's clothes still hanging on the peg, and a black bloodstain on the floor. When he tried to remove the clothes from the peg, they crumbled to dust."

This statement, if true, as it may well be, disposes of the belief, still held by some, that the garments in which the Red Fox died

[1] *The Book of Barcaldine*, by the Rev. A. Campbell Fraser (MacLehose: 1936).

Ruin of James of the Glen's earlier home, near the head of Glen Duror of Appin

The Narrows at Ballachulish, where the ferry plies. To the left lies Loch Linnhe : to the right the entrance to Loch Leven. Across the water is North Ballachulish. The knoll above the shore-line, on this side of the ferry, is the Gallows Hill, on which James of the Glen was hanged in 1752

Cairn on the moor above the Lettermore, denoting the spot where the Red Fox fell. The hills on the opposite shore of Loch Linnhe are those of Ardgour, to the right, and Morven, to the left

Acharn, in Glen Duror of Appin. The building on the right, now used as a steading, was the home of James of the Glen at the time of his arrest and imprisonment

are reverently preserved in Argyll. But there is no reason why we should not believe the stain at Glenure House to be his bloodstain.

Not so long ago, while Miss MacKay, afore-named, and two friends were driving along the road to Glenure House, they heard a Campbell lament, played on the pipes by a phantom piper. This, she tells me, was on May, 15th, the anniversary of the day on which Colin Campbell's body was carried home along this very road.[1]

[1] "I with two others, one a Breadalbain Campbell", Miss MacKay writes me in confirmation of this, just as we go to press, "certainly heard pipes being played, while driving along the road to Glenure House. My brother played the pipes, and had the loan of a set belonging to Campbell of Balliveolan. But he did not play the pipes that day, and we never could trace the player.

"On mentioning the incident later to Sir Duncan Campbell of Barcaldine and Glenure, he asked the date. It was 15th May. He then remarked : ' On that date Glenure's body would have been carried home. He was killed on the 14th.' "

# CHAPTER SIX

### THE PASS OF CORRIEYARRICK

IF, instead of following the Great North Road from Dalwhinnie to Newtonmore, you turn your steps due north, you tread the first stretch of the great highway built by General Wade between Dalwhinnie and Fort Augustus, in his endeavour to establish a direct means of communication for wheeled traffic between Badenoch and Lochaber. This is the road traversing that famous mountain-pass known as the Corrieyarrick. It leaves the Great North Road about a mile to the north of the railway station at Dalwhinnie, and attains an altitude of 1,258 feet ere it descends to Cat Cleugh, or Cat Lodge, as it appears on the map. In order to facilitate the passage of troops and supplies between Ruthven Barracks and Fort Augustus, Wade constructed an additional road between Cat Cleugh and a point on his main road before it is carried across the River Truim, thus eliminating what otherwise would have been a considerable detour by Dalwhinnie. This latter road runs by Caraldie, and skirts the north-eastern flank of the mountain known as Gruban Beag. Much of it, to this day, is quite passable. From the junction of these roads he carried his Corrieyarrick highway on to Drumgask. The next mile or so is absorbed in what to-day is the highroad to Laggan. Thereafter it emerges in a field, is borne across the Mashie Water in Strath Mashie, and travels westward on the south side of the upper reaches of the Spey, passing by Shirrabeg and Shirramore, Garvabeg and Garvamore. At Garva Bridge it crosses the Spey. This double-arched structure, completed by Wade in 1732, is sometimes referred to as St. George's Bridge. It is roughly 150 feet in length; and each of its arches spans 40 feet to the centre pier, standing on a rock in the middle of the Spey.

Wade's great road now runs westward by Meallgarbha, beyond which it cuts into the Forest of Corrieyarrick, and in zigzag fashion ascends the Pass of the same name, keeping to the right of the stream called the Yarrick. Originally, the steep ascent to the summit of the Pass was achieved by seventeen traverses, each measuring 70 to 80 yards in length. Later, the number was reduced to thirteen. Robert Chambers, in his great work, *The History of the Rebellion of 1745*, gives a vivid description of Wade's road at this point when it consisted of seventeen traverses, "each of which leads the traveller but a small way forward in the actual course of his journey". A stone buttress some 10 to 15 feet in height retained each traverse on its outward side; while a drain or water-course was constructed on the inward side.

Little did General Wade imagine, when building his road over the Corrieyarrick, that it was ever likely to be of service to the Jacobites in the moving of *their* troops, or that the ditch constructed along the side of it might afford so many positions of secure entrenchment for the very rebels whose warlike activities this highway was designed to curtail! It was held that a small band of resolute men, well supplied with food and ammunition, could have cut off and entirely vanquished an army approaching these traverses, irrespective of its numbers or appointments.

Equally little did the Highlanders imagine that, before very long, they were to put Wade's roads and bridges to useful purpose! The road-making and bridge-building enterprises of this period were received throughout the Scottish Highlands with the greatest hostility—to begin with. Most of the chiefs and their clansmen regarded the General's engineering activities as a serious encroachment upon their liberties. Among the several grounds upon which they resented them was the obvious one that they would render their territories open to the intrusion of strangers, and thus deprive them of the security that, hitherto, the mountains had afforded them in time of invasion. The chiefs also claimed, according to Edward Burt, that the coming of strangers among them threatened to "destroy or weaken that attachment of their vassals, which it is so necessary for them to support and preserve".

"The middling order", Burt continues, "say the roads are to them an inconvenience instead of being useful, as they have turned them out of their old ways; for their horses being never shod, the gravel would soon whet away their hoofs, so as to render them unserviceable; whereas the rocks and moor-stones, though together they make a rough way, yet considered separately, they are generally pretty smooth on the surface where they tread. . . . The lowest class, who many of them at some times cannot compass a pair of shoes for themselves, allege that the gravel is intolerable for their naked feet; and the complaint has extended to their thin brogues. It is true they do sometimes for these reasons go without the road, and ride or walk in very incommodious ways."

But, much as the Highlanders railed against the roads, they railed even more against the bridges. The chiefs held that they would surely make the people effeminate, and incapable of crossing rivers and streams without artificial aid.

\* \* \* \* \*

Wade's road over the Corrieyarrick attains, at its highest point, an altitude of over 2,500 feet above sea-level. From the summit of the Pass it falls steeply through the watershed of the River Tarff. There used to be an ancient bridge just where it arrives at the tributary stream of the Tarff known as the *Allt Lagan a' Bhainne*, Brook of the Milky Hollow; but several years ago this bridge became quite impassable. As the crossing-place here is by no means safe, especially in time of torrent, a band of voluntary bridge-builders set-to in 1932, under the auspices of the Scottish Rights of Way Society, and constructed another bridge at this point, thus maintaining this arduous journey over the Corrieyarrick in a state of comparative safety for those traversing these mountain fastnesses out of sheer love for them. Beyond this bridge Wade's road runs northward through Glen Tarff to Fort Augustus and Loch Ness, passing by Cullachy House.

Wade was exceedingly proud of his Corrieyarrick road, although the cost of construction exceeded by nearly £300 the sum of £3,000 advanced to him for the purpose. The account rendered by him for this expenditure is to be found among the Treasury Papers. It was submitted to the Right Honourable Sir Robert Walpole and the Lords Commissioners of His Majesty's Treasury. This "Memoriall of Leut-Genll George Wade Sheweth:

"That by His Majesty's Warrant bearing date the 10th day of Aprill, 1731, the said Leut-Genll did receive from the Paymaster-Genll of His Majesty's Forces the Sum of Three Thousand pounds (subject to the usual deduction of poundage) in advance and upon Account of the Charge of carrying on the New Road for Wheel Carriage from the New Fortress of Fort Augustus to joyn the great Road made in the Preceding Years from

Crieff to Inverness, and for Building Stone Bridges where they should be found necessary.

"That the said Leut-Genll having provided the Stores and Materialls for carrying on the Work, did employ Seven Commission Officers and 348 Non-Commission Officers and Soldiers, who began in the Month of Aprill, and continued to work until the last day of October, during which time they perform'd 162 Days' Work; To this Number in the beginning of July were added 162 as before Non-Commission Officers and Soldiers who from that time to the end of October perform'd 103 Dayes Work; The whole Number Amounting to 510 Men besides Officers were paid at the Rates as usuall Viz: The Serjeants One Shilling, the Corporalls and Drummers at Eightpence, and the Soldiers at Sixpence pr diem, over and above their pay as Soldiers, and to those who were employed as Artificers, being Carpenters, Smiths, Miners, and Paviors, One Shilling pr diem was allowed them for working at their respective trades.

"He begs leave farther to Represent That the Said New Road is about 28 Measured Miles in length, and made through a part of the Country that was Scarcely passable for Man or Horse, being carried over the Coriarick Mountain (one of the highest in the Highlands) to Fort Augustus, and is now made as easy and practicable for Wheel Carriage as any Road in the Country.

"He begs leave likewise to Represent to Your Lordships That he has caused to be Erected on the Said Road Five Stone Bridges, one of which is built over the River Spey, consisting of two large Arches and is 180 Foot in length. The other four are of One Arch each and of smaller Dementions.

"The Said Roads and Bridges with all the Incident Charges attending so extensive a Work Amounts in the Whole to the Sum of £281, 4s. 8d. more than the Net Produce of His Majesty's Warrant as may appear by the particulars hereunto Annexed.

"He therefore humbly desires Your Lordships will be pleased to move His Majesty that he will be Graciously pleased to Grant a Warrant for the Payment of the Said Sum of £281, 4s. 8d., as also to prevent his being put in super for the Money's advanced by the Warrant Above mentioned.

"All which is most Humbly Submitted to your Lordships Concideration."

And now follow the details of expenditure as submitted by Wade in his Memorial to the Lords Commissioners. This "Account of Wages & Other Incident Charges in Carrying on the Work" is an interesting specimen of early eighteenth-century book-keeping:

| | | | | | | | |
|---|---|---|---|---|---|---|---|
| 15 Serjeants at One Shilling pr Diem, | . | . | . | . | £0 | 15 | 0 |
| 20 Corporalls and Drummers at 8d. pr Diem, | | . | . | | 0 | 13 | 4 |
| 25 Artificers at One Shilling pr Diem, | . | . | . | | 1 | 5 | 0 |
| 288 Soldiers at 6d. pr Diem, | . | . | . | . | 7 | 4 | 0 |
| 348 | | | | | £9 | 17 | 4 |

Paid to the above Numbers 162 Days at £9, 17s. od. pr
Diem, . . . . . . . . . £1598 8 0

Added to the Work in the Beginning of July:
3 Serjeants at One Shilling pr Diem, . . . . £0 3 0
10 Corporalls and Drummers at 8d. pr Diem, . . 0 6 8
5 Artificers at One Shilling pr Diem, . . . . 0 5 0
144 Soldiers at 6d. pr Diem, . . . . . . 3 12 0

162 £4 6 8

Paid to the Above Numbers 103 Days at £4, 6s. 8d. pr
Diem is . . . . . . . . . £446 6 8

### INCIDENT CHARGES

Paid to the Commission Officers for their attendance at
Work, . . . . . . . . . £170 0 0
Paid for Ten Cart Horses with harness and for repairing
Carts and Forges, . . . . . . . 120 0 0
For Artificers Tools, Timber and Sea Coal for the Travelling
Forges, . . . . . . . . . 80 0 0
For the Carriage of 6 months Provisions and Stores for 510
Workmen, . . . . . . . . 130 0 0
For Forrage, charge of building hutts, Firing and Medicenes
for Men, . . . . . . . . . 120 0 0
For Building Five Stone Bridges one of Two Arches and 4 of
one Arch, . . . . . . . . 466 0 0
For Deduction of Poundage of £300, . . . . 150 0 0

Advanced on Account, . . . . £3281 4 8

Advanced by His Majesty's Warrant of 3rd of Aprill 1731, £3000 0 0

Ballance due, £281 4 8

\* \* \* \* \*

That Wade in his time was regarded as a personage of some
importance is shown by the fact that the National Anthem had a
fourth verse which ran:

> *God grant that Marshall Wade*
> *May by Thy mighty aid*
> *Victory bring!*
> *May he sedition hush,*
> *And like a torrent rush*
> *Rebellious Scots to crush:*
> *God save the King.*

About a hundred years ago the Corrieyarrick road began to fall into disuse. J. B. Salmond in his admirable volume, *Wade in Scotland*, informs us on the testimony of a native of Dalwhinnie, whose father resided at Garvamore, that 1890 was the last year in which horses were brought over this famous Pass to the Falkirk Trysts, that cattle were driven over it until 1896, and sheep until 1899.

At Dalchully, not far from Drumgask, where, as I already have told you, about a mile of Wade's road is absorbed in the present highway to Laggan, you will see a picturesque Roman Catholic chapel set among fir-trees by the roadside, erected by the MacNabs of Dalchully. At Garvamore there is a keeper's house, which used to be an inn—evidence of the number of people wont to travel in olden times, either on foot or on horseback, or even by coach, over the Corrieyarrick.

★   ★   ★   ★   ★

Many travellers have left records of their adventures and experiences when crossing this Pass. In the winter of 1819 Father Donald Forbes, whose work was so closely associated with the chapel at Dalchully, made a trying passage over it, accompanied by four men and a pony. So inclement was the weather, and so deep lay the snow, that they all lost their way. They eventually reached their destination by allowing the pony to pick out the route. One of their number held on firmly to the pony's tail, while the remainder of the party followed behind in single file, each man holding the hand of the man in front of him.

Included in *Chambers's Domestic Annals of Scotland* is a letter written by a certain N. MacLeod, describing a journey through the Pass in 1731. The letter was published in a contemporary newspaper; and Chambers believes its author to have been none other than MacLeod of Dunvegan.

" Upon entering into a little glen, lately called Laggan a Vannah, but now by the soldiers Snugburgh, I heard the noise of many people, and saw six great fires, about each of which a number of soldiers was busy. During my wonder at the cause of this, an officer invited me to drink their majesties' healths. I attended him to each fire, and found that these were the six working-parties of Tatton's, Montague's, Mark Ker's, Harrison's, and Handyside's regiments, and the party from the Highland Companies,

119

making in all about five hundred men, who had this summer, with indefatigable pains, completed the great road for wheel-carriages between Fort Augustus and Ruthven. It being the 30th of October, his majesty's birthday, General Wade had given to each detachment an ox-feast, and liquor; six oxen were roasted whole, one at the head of each party. The joy was great, both upon the occasion of the day, and the work's being completed, which is really a wonderful undertaking."

\*     \*     \*     \*     \*

One of the most fascinating accounts of a journey through the Pass of Corrieyarrick is that published in 1799 by the Hon. Mrs. Murray of Kensington, and contained in her book, *A Guide to the Beauties of Scotland, &c., to which is added a more Particular Description of Scotland, especially that part of it called the Highlands.* In 1798 Mrs. Murray travelled through this desolate mountain-pass by coach, having set out from Kensington in May, 1796, with a maid by her side, and a footman seated behind her. The real name of this adventurous lady was Mrs. Aust. It appears, however, that for most purposes she preferred to retain the title bestowed upon her by a previous husband, the Hon. William Murray, brother of the Earl of Dunmore. At the age of fifty-two she travelled to Scotland by coach, resolved to explore the remoter regions of the Highlands. The coach was specially built to withstand the inordinate wear and tear involved in an expedition to the Highland hills in those days. The account she has left us of her experiences makes most thrilling reading. Sarah Aust is certainly deserving of a place among the more interesting and unusual travellers through Scotland in olden times; and a perusal of her *Guide* shows her to have been a woman of considerable character and courage.

That she had given some serious consideration to the arrangements one should make when embarking on a project as risky and as arduous as was an excursion through the Highlands at the end of the eighteenth century is evident from the advice she proffers as a preface to her account:

"Provide yourself with a strong roomy carriage, and have the springs well corded; have also a stop-pole and strong chain to the chaise. Take with you linch-pins and four shackles which hold up the braces of the body of the carriage; a turnscrew fit for fastening the nuts belonging to the shackles; a hammer and some straps. For the inside of the carriage get a light flat box, the corners must be taken off, next the doors for the more conveniently getting in and out. This box should hang on the front of the chaise, instead of the pocket, and be as large as the whole front, and as deep as the size of the carriage will admit: the side next the travellers should fall down by hinges at the height of their knees to form a table on their laps; the part of the box below the hinges should be divided into holes for wine bottles to stand upright in. The part above the bottles to hold tea, sugar, bread and meat; a tumbler glass, knife, fork, and salt cellar, with two or three napkins; the box to have a very good lock. I would also advise to be taken, bed-linen, and half a dozen towels at least, a blanket, thin quilt, and two pillows."

Only once during an itinerary extending to about two thousand miles did Mrs. Murray's carriage give her any trouble. When passing by Loch Awe in a rain-storm, the shackle attached to one of the rear springs broke. Disaster was averted by the promptitude with which the postillion brought the vehicle to a standstill. So vivid is her description of the journey over the Corrieyarrick that one need make no apology for quoting extensively from it:

"As we were sitting at breakfast with the good Governor of Fort Augustus, an Oxonian sent in his name, begging leave to see the fort. He had permission, and was invited to breakfast; he was a very genteel young man, and gave us some account of his tour. . . . At Dalwhinnie the road to Fort Augustus over Corryarraick branches from the great Inverness road. None of this young gentleman's party dared to encounter that road, except himself and servant, on horseback; the rest went on to Inverness by the great road. The day he crossed Corryarraick was a continued violent rain and storm of wind, which gave it the appearance of wild desolation, beyond anything he could describe; and the whole of the road itself, he said, was rough, dangerous, and dreadful, even for a horse. The steep and black mountains, and the roaring torrents, rendered every step his horse took, frightful; and when he attained the summit of the zigzag up Corryarraick, he thought the horses, himself, man and all, would be carried away, he knew not whither; so strong was the blast, so hard the rain, and so very thick the mist; and as for cold, it stupefied him. He thought it almost a miracle to escape unhurt from such horrid wastes, roaring torrents, unwholesome vapours, and frightful fogs; drenched from top to toe, frozen with cold, and half dead with fatigue. He said he had heard people had gone that pass in a carriage, but he was sure it was impossible. The governor's family assured him it was done frequently; and turning to me, said ' here is one who means to do so tomorrow, in a chaise'. The gentleman stared, and added, ' Then I must alter my journal, for I thought it impossible'. A young lady present said, she had crossed the mountain on horseback in winter, when snow was on the ground, but it was hazardous. Many, by imprudence, have there lost their lives in winter; and some indeed from fatigue and cold; particularly one poor woman, attending on a marching troop, carrying an infant in her arms. At the top of the mountain she sank, and would not be persuaded to be removed, nor suffer the child to be taken from her. She fell asleep, and the people who were sent the next morning from the fort to seek for her, found her sitting against a stone, nearly covered with snow. The woman was quite dead; but the infant at her breast, being entirely covered with snow, was not absolutely lifeless. It was carried to the fort, where the governor's lady (from whom I had this sad tale) restored it to life; but it did not recover the perfect use of its limbs for many weeks, so much were they frozen. Soldiers, too, in their march, have often perished there, by imprudently drinking quantities of spirits at the inn on the Moor, thinking thereby to keep out the cold; but alas! it was the sure way to destruction."

All these accounts did not deter Sarah Aust from attempting the Pass. She was determined to see it, and had returned from Fort William with this intention. Her postillion had been over it in May; and he thought that, though the road was bad and rough, he could drive her over it in safety, if she could procure an additional pair of horses. The smith carefully examined the carriage, putting right all that was wrong. At eight o'clock in the morning she took leave of her friends at the fort, and drove to the inn, where a couple of plough horses, harnessed with ropes, were added to her own. On reaching the bridge crossing the Tarff, she alighted, preferring the safety of her own legs to a reliance on the horses when negotiating the gorge.

Having arrived at the summit of the Pass, she again alighted to study the climate:

"It was certainly cold enough for my great coat; but I became neither torpid nor frozen. I discharged my plough horses. . . . When I came to the beginning of the zigzag, the sun began to shine; and to the south-west, above the rest of the mountain ocean's waves, I saw Ben Nivis, which I distinguished from the other mountains, it being rendered conspicuous by the sun shining upon its white patches of snow. At the commencement of the zigzag I got out of the carriage, and walked down at my leisure; amusing myself by picking up curious stones and pebbles in the channels made by the torrents, which cross the road at every five or ten yards. Round the base of the mountain, at some distance from the zigzag, is a stream, into which the other torrents dash; leaving behind them broad channels of smooth round stones, washed from the higher parts. The road is so cut up by these violent torrents, from the top of the zigzag to the entrance on the plain, that for four or five miles scarcely ten yards can be found free of them; which is, indeed, sufficient to pull a light carriage to pieces. Allen led the horses, and the wheels being dragged, he came quietly and safely to the bottom of that extraordinary pass. . . . I longed, but I longed in vain, for the effect of a moving zigzag, such as was described by my friend Major Barry. One part of the 24th Regiment, in which he served in the year 1746, was, on a fine sun-shining day, marching from Fort Augustus over Corryarraick. The officers, to add to the uncommonness of the scene, ordered the men to walk one by one down the zigzag; and the baggage and women to bring up the rear on horseback. What an extraordinary appearance in such a desert! To see a military moving zigzag of almost two miles; their arms glittering in the summer sunbeams, shining full upon them, and their officers at the bottom admiring the sight. I had not the pleasure of seeing a living being there, except the men and horses with the chaise, slowly creeping down the curious ridge: but in my mind's eye, I saw the Major's troops; I beheld their arms glitter; the women mounted, bringing up the rear; and he himself by my side, in raptures at the effect of their plan."

★　　★　　★　　★　　★

Prince Charlie, on his journey south, made for the Corrieyarrick from the direction of Aberchalder and Loch Oich. At the point at which he arrived at Wade's road, there is a grassy knowe surrounded by a trench, and known in Highland story as Prince Charlie's Dining-table. Tradition has it that at this spot Charlie and his officers tarried for a meal.

On August, 26th, 1745, Johnnie Cope came this way from Dalnacardoch, hoping to join warlike issue with the Jacobites on the Corrieyarrick. Charlie, on hearing that Cope's advance forces were encamped at Garvamore, was thrilled at the prospect. "Before I take off these brogues", he is said to have remarked with the greatest confidence as to the upshot, "I shall engage Mr. Cope!" But the Hanoverian general's outposts were still a goodly step from this formidable Pass when he decided, at Dalwhinnie, to alter his plans, and march north to Inverness instead. By the time that the Hanoverian army reached Dalwhinnie, Cope had received the news that the Jacobites were now 3,000 strong, that they were advancing to take possession of the Corrieyarrick, and that a band of Charlie's troopers was lying in wait by the bridge at Snugburgh, situated at one of the most perilous passages through this fastness. The design was to engage Cope's men at this point, while another Jacobite contingent marched swiftly round by a defile to the west, to cut off any possible line of retreat. This information was conveyed to Cope by a certain Captain Sweetenham, from whom the Hanoverian leader obtained the first definite news of the movements and strength of the Jacobite forces already mustered in Scotland. You may recall that, when Gordon of Glenbucket joined the Prince at Glenaladale, he brought Sweetenham with him. This English officer, a captain in Guise's Regiment, had been taken prisoner by the MacDonalds of Keppoch, while on his way between Ruthven Barracks and Fort William, and had actually witnessed the raising of the Jacobite Standard at Glenfinnan. He had been released on parole, with instructions to convey to Johnnie Cope a message of defiance from Prince Charlie.

Sweetenham's estimate of the Jacobites' numerical strength was certainly disturbing, since it was the computation of a man who, in the capacity of captive, had been afforded the singular opportunity of seeing for himself the Jacobite forces. His calculations were confirmed by a letter Cope received soon afterwards from Lord President Forbes, then in residence at Culloden House.

It is generally admitted that, had Cope carried out his original plan to penetrate westward in the direction of the Corrieyarrick, he and his men would have been vanquished, probably to a man. Notice of this danger caused him to think seriously at Dalwhinnie. So, on August, 27th, when the elated Jacobites were fully expecting him to fall into their mesh, he summoned a council of war to discuss an alternative move. On the inadvisability of advancing toward the Corrieyarrick there was unanimous agreement. It was also conceded that, since the Highlanders could penetrate south to the Lowlands by several other routes, there was nothing to be gained by delaying a moment longer in the neighbourhood of Dalwhinnie. Against the suggestion that Cope and his army should now retrace their steps southward, there was the obvious danger that in so doing they ran the risk of being cut off by the enemy, who were now in a position to intercept their retreat, or at any rate to harry them by the wholesale destruction of roads and bridges. Furthermore—and this was the most important consideration—the instructions given to Cope were so strongly in favour of an advance in a northerly direction, in the expectation that his army might encounter, and possibly rout, such forces of the Jacobites as held the northern field, that it would have left

Cope open to serious criticism from the Government, had he marched southward from Dalwhinnie. A move toward Inverness, therefore, seemed the only alternative. His council of war terminated in an agreement that Inverness was the only feasible course—an agreement as unanimous as had been the opinion that the intention to march over the Corrieyarrick to Fort Augustus should be abandoned. The circumstances necessitating this change of campaign were provoking to Cope, since he was alive to the importance of occupying the Great Glen at this point. Fort Augustus, as he well realized, was in easy communication with the other forts erected to curb the activities of the insurgents. In addition, it was situated on the margin of the territories occupied by the clans that were, perhaps, the most disaffected. So he continued northward by the road traversing Badenoch and the wild Grampians—the road referred to by Robert Chambers in his *History of the Rebellion* as being " so remarkable in the memory of all travellers for its lonely desolation in summer, and its dangerous character when the ground is covered with snow ". In the course of his march on Inverness, he entertained the prospect of having his force considerably augmented by accessions from the clans then described as loyal. Moreover, there was a feeling abroad among his officers that, since an advance in this airt threatened the homes and countryside of a considerable number of the Jacobites then under arms, they would think twice before hurrying south to occupy the lowlands when their own hearths now lay at the mercy of the Hanoverians.

At the time when orders were given to change the direction of march, the van of Cope's army had penetrated as far as Blairobeg, situated some three miles to the south of Garvamore, and less than a dozen miles from the Corrieyarrick. The rear of his army lay in the vicinity of Cat Cleugh, four miles behind. His poor troopers must have experienced something in the nature of dismay and disappointment when the order was given to turn about, and make for Inverness by the Barracks of Ruthven.[1] A

---

[1] On a green mound sprinkled with fir-trees, just across the Spey from Kingussie, are the ruins of Ruthven Barracks. The mound, which measures 60 feet in height, 360 feet in length, and 180 feet in width, is said to be artificial, and has every appearance of its being so. Prior to the building of the barracks upon it, this site was occupied by Ruthven Castle, a keep belonging to that desperado known to Scottish history as the Wolf of Badenoch. The Government purchased the mound in 1716. Eighteen years later, Wade constructed upon it " in a workmanlike and substantial manner a stable for 30 Dragoons

historian of the period tells us, incidentally, that "two rowan-trees mark the place where Sir John Cope's army faced about, and avoided an action with the rebels". The actual spot is still referred to by the shepherds and mountain-dwellers in these parts as Cope's Turn.

So as to deceive the Highlanders, whose scouts lay in vigilance among the heather in the upper reaches of the Corrieyarrick, Cope directed that a detachment of his forces should make a conspicuous advance toward the summit, as though it were the advance guard of an army about to attack. It was ordered that this ruse should be maintained until the main body of his army had been given time to cover half a day's march toward Inverness, whereafter it was expected to make up on the main body as best it could. By a series of forced marches, Cope and his army reached Inverness on August, 29th. Not a day's halt had they been permitted since they quitted Crieff on the 21st; and, were it not that a hundred horse-loads of bread left at Stirling had not come up in time, it is doubtful whether the army would have been allowed even the brief respite it enjoyed at Crieff.

with all conveniences thereunto belonging, together with a guard-house for the security thereof".

On more than one occasion Ruthven Barracks were besieged by the Highlanders for Prince Charlie. When Johnnie Cope moved northward in the autumn of 1745, he left them in the care of one, Sergeant Molloy, and no more than a dozen soldiers. This tempted the Jacobites to attack it. So, three hundred of them, under the leadership of Dr. Archibald Cameron and O'Sullivan, set out with this design. Molloy and his skeleton garrison successfully withstood the siege, however; and at length the Jacobites were obliged to withdraw.

Another attempt to take Ruthven was made by the Jacobites as they retreated toward the north in the spring of 1746. In February of that year, a considerable force, commanded by Gordon of Glenbucket, surrounded it and demanded capitulation. Since the Jacobites were strengthened on this occasion by several pieces of artillery, Molloy took the view that resistance would be futile. He, therefore, signified his willingness to surrender, provided the garrison would be permitted to evacuate the barracks, together with bag and baggage. Molloy and his men were escorted thence to the Blair of Atholl. "Insensible to their own advantages", as one chronicler puts it, the Jacobites now proceeded to blow up a building that might have proved very useful to them at a later stage in the Rebellion.

The view that Ruthven was constructed more for the purpose of housing troops than as a stronghold is supported by the fact that nowhere about it is there any trace of gun emplacements. For all that, it exhibited certain strategical advantages in the warfare of the period. Built about the same time, and almost to the same design, were the barracks at Bernera, in Glen Elg, calculated to keep in check the lawless clans of the West Highlands, particularly those located in Skye.

Following upon the rout of the Highlanders at Culloden, it was arranged that such of them as survived should convene at Ruthven. This they did. There they were presented with Prince Charlie's instruction that they should disperse, and obtain for themselves such safety as circumstances and the mountains offered.

The road to the Lowland plains and to Edinburgh now lay clear. As Cope pursued his own fate in the direction of Inverness, Prince Charlie's army, reinforced to the tune of 1,800 men by the arrival of the Grants of Glenmoriston and the MacDonells of Glengarry, moved down to the base of the Corrieyarrick. The Prince had been apprised of Cope's movements by one of the Camerons who deserted from the Hanoverians at Cat Cleugh. The Jacobite officers and men were for pursuit when they realized what had happened. But at a council of war, summoned on arrival at Garvamore, it was decided to let Johnnie Cope go his own way, and to make the most of his having left the Lowlands unprotected. And thus the Jacobite forces hurried southward through Badenoch and Atholl to occupy Edinburgh.

\*   \*   \*   \*   \*

Cope's decision to abandon his intended march by General Wade's road over the Corrieyarrick was by no means the last *he* was to hear of what is still regarded by many strategists and students of ' The Forty-five ' as a blunder of the first magnitude. There is little doubt that it afforded the Jacobites one of the most signal opportunities of carrying the Rising to the success they had contemplated, and for the achievement of which they had fought so desperately, and sacrificed so immeasurably. On the one hand, it left the south unguarded against the advance of the Prince's army : on the other, Cope's march to Inverness proved so useless from a recruiting point of view that many influential Hanoverians began to wonder whether he was not really a Jacobite at heart ! In London, as elsewhere, the Corrieyarrick débâcle remained the topic of the day for many months. It was hotly debated in all the inns and ale-houses of the south. No one could explain it. Everyone was suspicious of connivance, of collusion, of treachery. That the Corrieyarrick incident figured prominently at Cope's court-martial may be seen from the report of it published in 1749 under the following illuminating title :
*The Report of Proceedings and Opinion of the Board of General Officers on their Examination into the Conduct and Behaviour, and Proceedings of Lieutenant-General Sir John Cope, Knight of the Bath, Colonel Peregrine Lascelles and Brigadier-General Thomas Fowke, From the Time of the breaking out of the Rebellion in North-Britain in the Year*

*1745, till the Action at Preston Pans inclusive. Taken publickly in the Great Room at the Horse-Guards in the year 1746 with a Preface containing Reasons for this Publication, London. Printed for W. Webb, near St. Paul's. MDCCLIX.*

The purport of this publication, as is made plain in an editorial note, was to vindicate Johnnie Cope, who, in the estimate of the editor or compiler, had been maligned mercilessly and unduly. According to the document, Cope was at Dalwhinnie when he received advice that the Jacobites had taken up their position among the fastnesses of the Corrieyarrick, where they resolved to await his approach. On receipt of this advice, "after the most serious Deliberation, and maturely weighing the consequences of every other Measure, it was unanimously resolved in a Council of War to march towards Inverness. And that this last step may be viewed in its true Light, it is necessary to describe the road across the Mountain, whence it will appear how great the risk would have been of attempting the Passage."

And here occurs a description of the Corrieyarrick certainly worthy of reproduction, since it shows how formidable an obstacle this mountain-pass appeared to a campaigner in the middle of the eighteenth century :

" The South Side of the Corriarrick is of so very sharp an Ascent that the Road traverses the whole Breadth of the Hill seventeen times before it arrives at the Top. The Road in descending on the North Side is flank'd for a considerable Space by a Wood, and is crossed by a large Hollow, which is the Bed of a Torrent, and whose Banks are so extremely steep, that it is not passable but by a Bridge, which was possessed by the Rebels, and could have been broken down in a very short time, if they had found it necessary. From this description it is plain that a very small Force, who were Masters of this Hill, were capable of stopping or even defeating a considerable Army that should attempt to dislodge them. For each Traverse, in ascending, is commanded by that above it ; so that even an unarmed Rabble, who were posted on the higher ground, might, without exposing themselves, extremely harass the Troops on their March. Whence the attempting to force seventeen traverses, every one of them capable of being thus defended, was an Undertaking which it would have been Madness to have engaged in, with a Number inferior to the Highlanders from the Knowledge of the Country, their natural Agility, and their Attachment to Ambushes and Skirmishes, would, in this situation, have indulged their Genius, and would, doubtless, have proved most formidable Opponents. Besides, could it be supposed that by the Bravery of the Troops, or an Uncommon Share of Good Fortune, all these Passes had been cleared, and

The Spey at Dalchully, on Wade's road between Dalwhinnie and Fort Augustus, by way of the Corrieyarrick

St. George's Bridge, bearing General Wade's Dalwhinnie-Fort Augustus (Corrieyarrick) Road over the upper reaches of the Spey at Garvamore, was completed in 1732

Wade's bridge carrying his Corrieyarrick road across the Mashie Burn, a tributary of the Spey

Where Wade's military road between Dalwhinnie and Fort
Augustus is carried over the Yarrick, high up in the Pass of
Corrieyarrick

the Army had arrived on the Top of the Corriarrick, yet the Descent would have been still more hazardous, and, if the aforementioned Bridge was broken down, became absolutely impossible ; for then neither a Carriage, nor a Baggage Horse, could have crossed the Hollow."

Among the matters Cope was asked to explain at his court-martial were his reasons for not attempting to force his way through the Pass of Corrieyarrick, or, alternatively, for his not having remained at Dalwhinnie where, it was maintained, he might have observed the movements of the Jacobites. Or again why, if he deemed it inadvisable to delay longer at Dalwhinnie, he moved northward to Inverness, when he might have fallen back on Stirling. Cope's explanations are indeed instructive. "At Dalwhinnie I had intelligence that the rebels were then upwards of three thousand strong, at which time the whole force I had with me did not exceed fourteen hundred effective men— that the rebels were determined to meet the King's army at the several passes above Snugburgh, a place at the north side of the Corrieyarrick over which lay the direct road to Fort Augustus, and from which mountain there is another lying north of it, while another party of them was to march through a glen on the west side of the mountain to attack our rear after we entered the hill."

Cope maintained further that it was utterly impracticable, whilst the rebels lay there to oppose him, to force a passage over the Pass to Fort Augustus. To have attacked the Highlanders in so strong a position was to expose his troops to certain destruction. "It is true", he records, "we had two companies of Lord John Murray's Highland Regiment and a few of Lord Louden's, but numbers of them deserted every night with their arms, in so much that, of one of the companies which was complete when we begun our march, only fifteen remained when we marched into Inverness. . . . If the rebels intended to march south, we knew that it was not in our power to prevent them, for they had ways to march through the mountains to the westward of the Corrie-yarrick by roads that were practicable for Highlanders though not for regular troops with artillery and provisions, and that by the near route which they might take, and by their being able greatly to out-march the King's troops, they would get to Stirling before us."

Be all this as it may, Johnnie Cope unquestionably blundered when he resolved to move northward from Dalwhinnie. No more than a couple of hundred men joined his colours at Inverness; and these were almost exclusively men of the Clan Munro who, on the plea that their harvests would soon be ripe, had enlisted only for a week or two, and at the same time stipulated that, during their short term of service, they should receive a rate of pay higher than the standard rate.

Meanwhile Prince Charlie's army, unchecked, with Wade's roads and bridges now at its disposal, and flushed with a sense of having stolen a considerable march on the enemy, was overrunning the Lowland plains.

\*    \*    \*    \*    \*

It was not until the autumn of 1936 that I actually established some personal contact with the Corrieyarrick. One afternoon of warm, mellowing sunshine, as I sat poring over a map of the Central Highlands, spread out on a table at the window of my home in Chelsea, my eyes rested on the words, Pass of Corrie-yarrick. This, and the beckoning sunlight, revived in me that longing for the seas and the moors of Scotland, and a desire to gratify a wish I had entertained for many years—namely, to be able to say with the most adventurous of British travellers on foot that I had journeyed through this Pass. I now had the urge to satisfy myself that my long residence in London had not rendered me an effete Southron. That evening, with a ticket for Dalwhinnie in my pocket, I boarded at Euston a train northward bound. Early in the afternoon of the following day, I was seated in the Highland train leaving Buchanan Street, Glasgow, for Inverness and the north, and timed to deposit me about tea-time at Dalwhinnie, where I had arranged to pick up a mountaineering friend travelling in like manner through the Lairig Ghru to meet me, that we might launch our attack together on the traverses which, ever since the days of the Old Chevalier, have carried Wade's military road up the formidable face of the Corrieyarrick.

I duly picked up my friend; and, since an hour or two of daylight still remained after we had had a good Scots tea at a wayside hostelry in Dalwhinnie, we decided to reduce the following day's journey by setting out there and then in the direction of Cat

Cleugh and Laggan. Toward nightfall we sought the Manse at Laggan, and threw ourselves on the hospitality of my father's good friend, the late Rev. Dr. Neil Ross, minister of Laggan parish, and one of the few men of culture and erudition connected with the Celtic movement in Scotland in recent times.

It was 10 a.m. on the morrow ere we quitted the Manse for the fastnesses of the Corrieyarrick. The day was hazy and sultry. Having crossed the Spey, we followed a pleasing path flanking its southern bank for about a mile. Eventually we reached the Mashie Burn. Here I was tempted to photograph the old bridge Wade threw over this tributary of the Spey. A flock of sheep, grazing near at hand, lent a pastoral touch to the setting; and I confess to having spent some time in coaxing some of these black-faced creatures to present themselves to the lens of the camera. The road now passed under the shade of the wooded height known as the Black Craig, a site of interest to archaeologists because of the ancient hill-fort dominating it, but to-day re-presented by the merest ruin, high up among the pine-tree tops. Situated at the foot of the Black Craig, and likewise among pine-trees, is the Roman Catholic chapel alluded to earlier. The door of the chapel we found locked; but we peered in through its windows, and enjoyed, among the cool, shady pines, a few minutes' diversion from our track through the mountains, speculating in the meantime as to where lay the hiding-place of that eminent fugitive, Cluny MacPherson—Cluny of 'The Forty-five', as he is usually called. Cluny knew many a place of refuge among the Highland hills; and certainly the retreat to which he resorted in the neighbourhood of Dalchully was secure enough in those times.

Although the day was fine, it soon became obvious that it was not to be a day for landscape photography. Indeed, except for the photograph I took by the roadside close to the chapel, showing a stretch of the Spey, with the mountain known as Buidh Aonach in the background, no real opportunity of using the camera presented itself all that day. As we approached Glenshirra Lodge and the edge of Loch Crunachan, a few gluttonous minutes were spent in eating wild raspberries, and thereafter another minute or two in marvelling at the fields of scabious in full bloom, stretching ahead and away to the right of us. In profusion, not even the heather growing on the wilds penetrated by General Wade's road over the Corrieyarrick rivalled these acres of scabious.

Onward we swung at a steady pace, taking the road's gentle undulations in our stride until, at Garvamore, we halted by that lovely bridge Wade and his soldiers threw across the Spey in two spans. Here we exchanged the traveller's salutation with a lad pedalling past us from behind on a very light bicycle fairly well adapted to conditions such as these.

"Where do you think you're going on *that?*" I asked. this cheery fellow, in stepping aside to allow of his picking the best of a road noticeably degenerating every hundred yards or so.

"Tae Forrt Augustus, o' course!"

"What?" I continued. "Do you seriously propose riding that machine over the Corrieyarrick?"

"What for no? I cam ower the Lairig Ghru on it yesterday; an' Ah cannae see what way it shouldna tak' me doon Glen Tairff tae Forrt Augustus the day!"

Thus our fellow-traveller, whirring through this wild and broken country on two fragile wheels, passed on at a pace roughly thrice that of ours. My friend and I looked whimsically at one another. "Don't wish him any harm", we both said simultaneously; "but I hope he gets a puncture!" we added, uncharitably. However, it appeared as though no such annoyance had befallen him. If it had, he certainly rectified it with amazing alacrity, since we never saw him again, although, throughout the remainder of our journey, in the shape of tyre marks where spates had deposited shallow belts of soft silt and sand across Wade's road, high up among the mountains, we had recurring evidence of this lightsome passenger.

Midway between Garva Bridge and Meallgarbha we tarried to partake of such food as our knapsacks contained; and here I, with my incurable partiality for water in any form whatsoever, bathed my feet for some time in a cool, refreshing stream running at right angles to our track in its hurry to join the head-waters of the Spey, but a few hundred yards off. Near Meallgarbha, and perhaps a couple of hundred yards from the road, we again observed evidence of Wade's activities in the form of yet another bridge. Neither to nor from this beautiful little structure did as much as a pathway lead, showing that only in parts does the modern, vehicular road to Meallgarbha follow the line of Wade's military road. It was at Meallgarbha that, without a doubt, the route now lying before us was the mountain-track into which Wade's double carriage-way has deteriorated. Broken and swept away in places by the storms and spates of the last two centuries, it leads up through the Pass of Corrieyarrick, following faithfully the alignment of the original military road, on the broken surface of which it lies. For the most part, it is now little more than a footpath, running for many miles through the centre of a road, much of which remains exactly as it must have been during the third and fourth decades of the eighteenth century, except for the fact that it is almost completely mossy and grass-grown. Much of the stone-work and retaining walls was undisturbed; and here and there, along this wild and ancient highway, one saw gravel-pits excavated during the course of its construction, and even heaps of road-metal, broken two centuries ago by Hanoverian soldiery for surfacing and repairing purposes.

At Meallgarbha a track, some five miles in length, strikes off in a south-westerly direction toward that small, remote lake among the mountains known as Loch Spey, whence originates the famous river of the same name. In optimistic mood at the outset of our journey, we had entertained a vague notion of leaving our knapsacks by the edge of Wade's road, and of hurrying along this track merely with our cameras. But it soon became patent that an additional ten miles or so at this juncture would have been foolish, when we still had before us so much arduous climbing, and Fort Augustus, our destination, still a very long way off.

Looking back through the length of the glen we had just traversed, little could be discerned with clearness, except the pine-woods by Garvamore, since the land was overcast with a vibrating haze, through which the mountains showed but dimly. For me, this was the most disappointing feature of the day. The long climb; the weight of my knapsack, largely on account of photographic paraphernalia; the oppressive heat; the pain of sunburn in arms and neck; the need for hurry against approaching darkness—all these, and more, one could have endured with some fortitude and philosophy. But a day of indifferent visibility was intolerable.  Of all the regions of Scotland, there are few in which I was more anxious for conditions favourable to panoramic photography.  That great mountain mass to the south, dominated by Creag Meaghaidh, might have been part of a mirky sky.  Of the incomparable view of the Monadhliath's flanks, shedding their waters toward the valley of the Spey, nothing at all could be seen from the heights of the Corrieyarrick.

\*     \*     \*     \*     \*

Before we reached the zigzags carrying Wade's road up the steepest gradients of the Pass, I discovered great clusters of cranberry and bilberry plants, the fruit upon them unnoticed as yet by grouse and other species of moorland fowl that soon strip such plants of their berries, once they have located them.  For several minutes my friend and I worked assiduously with fingers and jaws among these clusters.  As we arrived at the first of the zigzags, I proceeded to take what atmospheric conditions determined should be the last photograph for that day—the old bridge bearing Wade's road over the mountain rill known as the Yarrick, with much of the *coire* or corrie of the same name rising precipitously in the background.  The next three-quarters of an hour were devoted to what we regarded as the only serious piece of climbing throughout the entire journey.  Instead of following the ascending road through all its windings and contortions, we took the short and very steep strips of footpath running straight up the face of the Pass, regardless of zigzag or traverse.  By about 4.30 p.m. we attained the summit, at 2,507 feet above sea-level.  Save for the voice of a solitary ptarmigan, the summit seemed devoid of life.  As we trudged on through the flat and exposed territory surrounding it, a fresh wind, blowing in our faces from the west, now assisted in removing the beads of perspiration brought forth by the exertions demanded on a day so sultry by the steepness of the climb.  This unfrequented stretch of Scotland certainly bore the aspect of sterility and wilderness.  Had it not been for the pervading haze, the view to the west would have been one where peaks and ridges, rising behind one another in endless sequence, carried the eye far into the heart of that mountainous country known in olden times as the Rough Bounds of Scotland, because of its wildness and inaccessibility. What photographs of mountain scenery we would have taken from the summit of the Pass, but for bad visibility!

One distinctly felt an eeriness about the summit—a definite sense of its being haunted, not merely by the shepherd who, they say, walks the Pass with his collie, putting to everyone he meets the question, "*C'aite am bheil thu dol?*" (Where are you going?). I have mountaineering friends who firmly believe they have been spoken to by the phantom shepherd; and they assure me further that, when approaching the summit, either from the east or from the west, their dogs, contrary to the usual behaviour of their kind in such circumstances, exhibited a weird apprehension, which restrained them from running on ahead. However, once the summit was passed, any such fear seemed to disappear. The descent to Fort Augustus was gradual and regular on the whole. The last of the Wade bridges, and perhaps the most picturesque, was that conveying the General's road over the stream deriving its sustenance from Cullachy Forest, and from the western watershed of the Pass itself. By this bridge we lingered awhile; and I regretted that at the time the sun was at least two hours' journey from the point at which it might have made this bonnie spot reproducible. There seemed no purpose in tarrying. Already at this season of year the sun was at an altitude indicating with certainty that in two hours' time it would have sunk out of sight behind the hills.

By no means as attractive was the bridge erected at *Lagan a' Bhainne*, the Milky Hollow, by the Scottish Rights of Way Society, though it served its purpose admirably enough, and demonstrated, on a moment's acquaintance with it, that, without it, this deep ravine, carrying an impetuous tributary to the River Tarff, would have presented a formidable problem, especially to a tired wayfarer making for Fort Augustus and some modicum of civilization again, at the close of an arduous day.

The Milky Hollow, by the way, has its share of historic association. It was at this spot, as noted earlier, that two working parties met in 1731, and celebrated the completion of this military road with much liquor, and with six oxen roasted on six huge fires. Here, also, you may recollect, Prince Charlie tarried the night, before crossing the Pass with his army.

Where the track bends round into Glen Tarff, the wayside was gladdened by moorland flowers innumerable. Most conspicuous among them in the waning light was that beautiful, chaste handiwork of God, the waxen grass-of-Parnassus. Obviously, we suddenly had descended to an altitude at which prevailing winds and temperatures favoured the growth of the less hardy species of flowering plants. Far ahead, and well below us, lay a fading corner of Loch Ness. We were now approaching the gentler parts of the glen, where the Tarff runs through territory less austere, and attractively wooded. A slight incline brought us by Cullachy House; and by nightfall our feet were on the main highway once more, within a mile or two of Fort Augustus.

When, an hour or so later, we sat down to a meal in a wayside cottage on the outskirts of the village, I felt as though, at last, something memorable had been accomplished—as though, at long last, I had achieved one of the major ambitions of my life!

Behind us now, wrapped in darkness and silence, lay that wild highway of an age that is gone. More than two centuries have passed since the Red-Coats hewed their carriage-way through the Corrieyarrick's desolation; and just two centuries have drifted by since a luckless Prince harried his enemies from the very traverses built in an endeavour to control the seditious activities of those in rebellion on his behalf. Yet, the Pass of Corrieyarrick retains its sough of 'The Fifteen' and 'The Forty-five'. Here one should *expect* to encounter the old, grey ghosts of the ancient fighters, claymore in hand.

# CHAPTER SEVEN

## ROTHIEMURCHUS

### AN ANCIENT HIGHLAND HERITAGE

ON the shelf that my father reserved for the more intimate of his books stood a copy of the first edition of the *Memoirs of a Highland Lady*, that fascinating autobiography of Elizabeth Grant of Rothiemurchus, covering the years between 1797 (her birthyear) and 1830, edited by Lady Strachey, and published by John Murray. I had not been born when the first edition made its appearance in 1898; and I was still a long way from being able to read when my father, anxious that I should have some knowledge of Highland domestic matters, considered it his duty to read aloud to me, from time to time, certain passages from the *Memoirs* which he believed would interest me in that direction. In addition to this, Grant of Rothiemurchus, then sheriff at Inverness, was his friend and contemporary; and, so, scarcely a week went by in our Highland home without some mention of the Grants, or of the Doune, the ancestral hearth in the heart of their pine-sown heritage stretching from the banks of the Spey to the foothills of the Cairngorms. Thus the name, Rothiemurchus, carries me back as far as I can remember.

Yet another association, almost lifelong, have I with Rothiemurchus: I have never forgotten that photograph of the ruined keep on an islet in Loch-an-Eilein, still to be found in Hume Brown's *Short History of Scotland*, a text-book I was obliged to study as a schoolboy at Edinburgh. I knew that Loch-an-Eilein lay in Rothiemurchus, though Hume Brown never mentions the name. This fragment of information I had derived from my father's faithful readings from the *Memoirs*. Hume Brown writes of the keep as having been the retreat of Alexander Stewart, Earl of Buchan, the lawless brother of King Robert of Scotland, and better known to Scottish historians as the Wolf of Badenoch.

For all practical purposes, Rothiemurchus and much of the territory impinging upon it remained a *terra incognita* to me until a decade or so ago, when there came into my hands an artistic brochure bearing on its front page a photograph of the Doune, deep-set among trees, and backed by mountains. Elsewhere in this brochure were sundry details about the locality, together with tariff figures in operation at the Doune, which, meantime, had been converted into a hotel. Printed under the photograph (and not too accurately) was that memorable passage from the *Memoirs of a Highland Lady*:

> "Tor Alvie on the right, Craigellachie before us, and our own most beautiful 'plain of the fir trees' opening out as we advanced, the house of the Doune appearing for a moment as we passed on by Lynwilg. We had as usual to go on to the big boat at Inverdruie, feasting our eyes all the way on the fine range of the Cairngorm, the pass of the Larrig between Cairngorm and Brae-Riach, the hill of Kincairn standing forward to the north to enclose the forest which spread all along the banks of the Spey, the foreground relieved by hillocks clothed with birch, fields, streams, and the smoke from the numerous cottages. Our beloved Ord Bain rose right in front, with its bald head and birch-covered sides, and we could point out our favourite spots to one another as we passed along, some coming into sight as others receded, till the clamour of our young voices, at first amusing, had to be hushed. We were so happy! we were at last come home; London was given up, and in our dearly loved Rothiemurchus we now fully believed we were to live and die."

This passage induced me to read the *Memoirs* for myself; and, the more I read, the more I became convinced that this was not merely one of the most faithful pictures of life in the Highlands during the opening years of the nineteenth century, but also one of the most fascinating narratives of its kind in the English language. I now resolved to repair a long-standing omission by a visit to the Doune, and by calling on John Peter Grant of Rothiemurchus, who, by this time, had succeeded his father as sheriff at Inverness, and still resides at Rothiemurchus, not far from the Doune. It was an interesting experience, this visit to Rothiemurchus. Nothing surprised me about it, except perhaps, that I could scarcely believe the western confines of this ancient Highland heritage were so near Aviemore, a district through which I had travelled oftener than I could remember, unaware that parts of Rothiemurchus lay within half an hour's walk of it.

\* \* \* \* \*

Wendy Wood, author of that delightful book, *The Secret of Spey*, has aptly described Loch-an-Eilein as the show-place of Rothiemurchus. This beautiful sheet of water is overlooked by the mighty range of the Cairngorms. Three-fourths of its shores, right down to the water's edge, are fringed with pines. The extent and density of these pines, forming what is known as the Forest of Rothiemurchus, encircling, as it does, the major portion of the loch, and stretching eastward to Loch Morlich and Glen-more Forest, would be difficult to imagine for anyone unaccustomed to landscapes of this nature. Sweeping away and away beyond Loch-an-Eilein, until they reach an altitude on the northern flanks of the Cairngorms, above which they find it hard to survive in any numbers, are the celebrated pines of Rothiemurchus. I doubt whether in Britain there is to be found so extensive an area covered with pines sown by nature; and there can be few panoramas more inspiring than that from the birchen crags of the Ord Ban, which includes the loch with its islet and ruined keep, the dense pine forests stretching far beyond, and one of the finest views of the Cairngorm range, the cairn-crowned summit of Cairngorm itself rising in ageless serenity to the skyline.

Rothiemurchus embraces a goodly portion of Cairngorm territory. In fact, most of the famous mountain-pass known as the Lairig Ghru lies in Rothiemurchus. The pass ceases to be Rothiemurchus to the south of the watershed, where it becomes Mar. Until the completion of the Highland Railway between Perth and Inverness in 1864, all the cattle of Rothiemurchus and of the surrounding country were herded through the Lairig Ghru to the marts at Braemar. With the advent of steam transport, this mountain-pass, from the point of view of droving, fell almost into complete desuetude. Up till that time, however, the Lairig route was regarded as being so important that, early every summer, a party of men from Rothiemurchus and the neighbouring localities made an excursion to it, in order to clear away stones and boulders deposited by the storms and spates of the previous winter, thus to facilitate the droving of cattle and sheep to the summer and autumn marts.

Judging by the density of the pines still comprising the Forest of Rothiemurchus, it is not easy to conceive what this estate must have resembled prior to the great timber fellings in 1862 and 1863, designed to provide sleepers for the Highland Railway, then in course of construction. Hitherto, the Spey was the sole means of transporting timber felled locally. There was a fair amount of shipbuilding at Inverness in those days. Much of the timber used in this enterprise was obtained from the Glenmore Forest, which borders Rothiemurchus on the north-east, and formed part of the Gordon Estates until purchased by the Forestry Commission about twenty years ago. This timber, when trimmed, was floated down the Spey. When the timber rafts reached Garmouth, at the river's mouth, the great oars or 'sweeps', used in steering them, were sold locally; and the revenue accruing therefrom was regarded for many years as a perquisite in the nature of pin-money for the wife of the Laird of Rothiemurchus.

Of interest, too, while we are on the matter of timber, is the fact that, about 1765, in the time of Patrick Grant, the White Laird, Rothiemurchus supplied London with water-pipes—the first water-pipes the metropolis ever had! They were of Scots firs, hewn at Rothiemurchus, and hollowed out at the boring-mill situated about a mile from the Doune. Great quantities of these firs were floated down the Spey to Garmouth, whence they were shipped direct to London. The southern end of the business was attended to by Dr. William Grant, younger brother of the White Laird, and great-great-great-grandfather of the present Laird. Dr. Grant resided in Lime Street, where he built up a flourishing practice. But for the unbusiness-like behaviour of the White Laird, this water-pipe enterprise would have gone from strength to strength. Correspondence still preserved at the Doune shows that, in the water-pipe industry as affecting London, the Rothiemurchus pines had no serious rival except a limited supply of elms procurable nearer at hand.

\* \* \* \* \*

Just below Loch-an-Eilein Cottage, which to-day functions as a tea-room for the scores of visitors finding their way here from Aviemore in the holiday season, is the point at which the keep associated with the Wolf of Badenoch is nearest the shore. The very pine-trees flanking the illustration in Hume Brown are there. Strange it was to look between their trunks at the ruined stronghold, and realize that they had not altered since my school-days at George Watson's College!

But, curiously, there appears to be not a tittle of evidence that the Wolf ever so much as set foot on the islet in Loch-an-Eilein. The story of his association with it seems to have been invented either by Sir Walter Scott, or by Sir Thomas Dick Lauder. The probability is that there has been some confusion between the stronghold in Loch-an-Eilein and that in the less picturesque Loch-in-dorb. So it would seem as though Hume Brown had perpetuated a fiction!

This ruined keep is said to have been one of the last nesting-places, in Scotland, of the osprey. But it is now many years, I am assured locally, since an osprey was seen in Rothiemurchus, or among the Cairngorm forests. That eminent Scottish natur-alist, Seton Gordon, mentions in his admirable book on the Cairngorms that ospreys nested upon the walls of the keep until 1900. And so tame were they that they sometimes perched on the chimney-tops of the dwelling already referred to as Loch-an-Eilein Cottage.

According to local tradition, three ospreys arrived at Loch-an-Eilein one spring. Two of them fought fiercely for a long time, until at length one bird managed to hold the other beneath the water and drown it! Although this species no longer nests in the neighbourhood, I am told that ospreys are seen occasionally, travelling over the Cairngorms.

*　　*　　*　　*　　*

In the days when Rothiemurchus belonged to the Shaws, the Doune did not occupy its present site. At that time it stood on the crest of a mound shaped like an elongated boat, upturned, by the banks of the Spey, quite close at hand. Some are of the opin-ion that the site of the present Doune was chosen when, several centuries ago, the Shaws lost Rothiemurchus to the Comyns, and the latter reduced the original habitation to ruins by trans-ferring building material from it to the new site. Others contend that the original Doune was razed when Patrick, the first Grant of Rothiemurchus, came into possession of the property.

The Doune, as we know it to-day, is situated on level ground amid peaceful surroundings, with a broad prospect of greenery retreating away from its southern windows toward the Ord Ban, sprinkled in places with deciduous trees and pines, and bordered on the west by the Spey, where it runs slowly through long, dark pools toward Inverdruie and Aviemore. Hereabouts, stretches of the Spey are very lovely, especially in late autumn, when the air tends to have a sharp edge, and the leaves are reddening.

The oldest part of the Doune, much of the exterior wall of which is still visible, is indeed interesting. Over the lintel of the doorway in that part built about 1700 is a stone beautifully carved with the motto, "In God is al my Trest", together with various emblems and armorial bearings, and the date, 1597, and also the initials P. G. and I. G. This lintel-stone, the Laird tells me, came originally from Muckerach Castle, the ruins of which stand among trees above the highway between Carr-bridge and Dulnain-bridge. Also from Muckerach came the studded wooden door, with its large keyholes and its heart-shaped spy-hole. This door now forms part of the outhouse at the Doune used as a lamp-room.

In wandering through this Doune of thick walls and well-proportioned windows, one readily absorbs something of the atmosphere of those who inhabited it during the early years of the nineteenth century, and of whom Elizabeth Grant writes so fascinatingly. The entire place is permeated with a sense of veneration, and of things not very far off, but sufficiently far to be irretrievable—irretrievable in an altered age, amid a people with altered interests and an altered outlook. Old-fashioned oil lamps are still used in the spacious public rooms; and any day you may see, on the upper landing, rows of candles in simple candlesticks, preparatory to the coming of night, since neither oil nor yet electricity has displaced, in the bedrooms, this old-world type of luminant. In this age of glare, the candles of the Doune are surely one of its attractions. Yet, when wandering at times in a favourable wind through the vast Forest of Rothiemurchus, or about the Doune itself, you are reminded of your own century by the rumbling of the great L.M.S. trains, climbing northward by Aviemore and Slochd to Inverness, or speeding south by Kingussie and the Grampian pass of Drumuachdar to the Lowland plains, and to Euston.

Much of the furniture and fittings of the Doune are in harmony —the low armchair in a room near the turret, for example, shaped to accommodate the crinolined ladies of Victorian times; the carved Adam mantelpieces; the deep cupboards and presses. They all tend to diffuse an atmosphere of quiet and contentment. In the drawing-room stands the lacquered chest-of-drawers mentioned in the *Memoirs* as having been the receptacle in which the Rothiemurchus children kept their beads and shells. Also in the drawing-room is the overmantel from Browning's villa in Florence; while in the main hall may be seen the gilded Italian bath that arrived from Italy about the same time. On the piano one may find fragments of old music, and, perchance, an old song or two—Lord Henry Somerset's *Echo*, with Christina Rossetti's haunting words:

> *Come to me in the silence of the night,*
>   *Come in the speaking silence of a dream;*
> *Come with soft-rounded cheeks, and eyes as bright*
>   *As sunlight on a stream:*
> *Come back in tears, come back in tears,*
> *Oh memory, hope, love, of former years!*

The Doune, moreover, is full of family portraits, some of which are of persons referred to in the *Memoirs*, and are quite old—reminiscent of the age when landed families were wont to sit for itinerary artists. Standing on the dining-room mantelpiece is the record of an old and interesting transaction in respect of pictures of the Grant family, painted early in the eighteenth century:

"Accompt James Grant of Rothiemurchus
to
Richard Waitt Picture drawer

| | | |
|---|---|---|
| In (?) for Three pictours of your own at one pound five Shill per pice is . . . . . . | 03 15 00 |
| ittem for two pictours of your Ladies at one pound five Shill per pice . . . . . . | 02 10 00 |
| ittem for a pictour of your Son M$^r$ Patrick at one pound five Shill:gs . . . . . . | 01 05 00 |
| Ittem for a pictour of your Son M$^r$ George at one pound five Shill:gs . . . . . . | 01 05 00 |
| | Summa | 08 15 00 |

Rothiemurchus June the ninth 1726
Grants me to have received frome the Much Honoured James Grant off Rothiemurchus the above accompt and discharges the Same and all others as witness my hand.
R$^{ic.}$ Waitt."

\* \* \* \* \*

Within shouting distance of the Doune are the steadings and other buildings appurtenant to the Doune Farm. One day in late autumn, when all the corn-fields had been stripped bare, I meandered through the barn. The rattle created by the threshing of sheaves attracted my attention. Closer investigation found me confronted with the old-fashioned threshing-mill one sees so often in operation on our larger farms. It instantly conveyed me back to my childhood days in the Highlands, when travelling threshing-mills of this design, drawn by powerful and noisy traction-engines, toured the countryside and visited the farms, threshing each farmer's grain in rotation. Hitched on behind each mill, when moving from place to place, was the caravan, or bothy, in which lived the sooty men who drove the tractor and worked the threshing-machine. So as to expedite matters, it was the custom in those days for the workers attached to neighbouring farms, as also for the general inhabitants of the countryside, to lend a hand at the threshing, thus enabling the machine to move on sooner to the next farm requisitioning its services.

Nowadays little of the grain threshed at Rothiemurchus is ground into meal. The grain is used mostly in the feeding of livestock and poultry. Occasionally quantities of it are disposed of locally, in order to replenish the dwindling supplies in adjoining barns.

*　　*　　*　　*　　*

Separated from the Doune by a few hundred yards of luscious meadowland is the old, low-roofed Parish Church of Rothiemurchus, and the older burying-place associated with it, surrounded by a beech hedge, and visited at will by brown sheep which, as Wendy Wood puts it, seem to have borrowed their colour from the russet leaves. Any number of Grants lie buried here; and some beautiful headstones mark the earthly resting-place of the members of other clans and families. Over at the east side are the tombs of the Rothiemurchus lairds, prominent among them that of my father's good friend, Sheriff Grant. Here, too, are the graves of Patrick, the first Grant, who came from Muckerach, and of Patrick, the laird known as MacAlpine because of his amiable attitude toward the nameless and landless MacGregors. MacPhersons from Badenoch also lie here; and a tall elder-tree, heavy in clustering berries during October, fills

Loch-an-Eilein and part of the Forest of Rothiemurchus, with the Cairngorms in the background. In the foreground lies the ruined keep

*Photo. by Valentine, Dundee*

*Above :* The Doune of Rothiemurchus

*Below :* Five weird stones in the Kirkyard at Rothiemurchus

The Doune of Rothiemurchus, seen from the birch-clad slopes of the Ord Ban on a wirdy day. Immediately beyond the belt of trees in the middle-distance, and on the left, flows the Spey. The hills in the background are the Monadhliaths

The ruined keep in Loch-an-Eilein, Rothiemurchus, with the Cairngorms in the distance

the walled sepulchre of the Camerons who, years ago, tenanted the Croft of Rothiemurchus.

The most conspicuous object of interest in this ancient place of burial is the recumbent slab denoting the grave of Farquhar Shaw, who "led and was one of the 30 of his Clan who defeated the 30 Davidsons of Inverhavon on the North Insh of Perth 1390. He died 1405." Placed upon this slab are five quaint, cylinder-shaped stones, one at each of the four corners, the fifth in the centre. These five stones, according to tradition, appear and disappear with the flow and ebb of the fortunes of the Rothiemurchus Lairds; and they are said to share with certain Celtic bells, such as the Bell of Insh and Saint Finnan's Bell, the power of finding their way back to their proper place of repose when wrongfully removed. Dire misfortune is believed to overtake anyone meddling with them. The natives will not even touch them.

Situated within a foot of one another in this same kirkyard are two tombstones of similar design. One of these marks the grave of Robert Scroggie, footman to the Duchess of Bedford, whose husband, more than a century ago, rented the Doune for a time. According to the inscription, Scroggie "was accidentally drowned whilst bathing in the Spey on the 15th October 1830, aged 22 years".

The other stone denotes the burial-place of Robert Latham, a native of Staffordshire, footman to the Marchioness of Abercorn. In August, 1837, at the age of twenty-three, he, too, was accidentally drowned in the Spey, near at hand.

Now, it was held locally that both of these footmen had met an untimely end through their having tampered, at one time or another, with one or more of the five queer, kebbuck-like stones on Farquhar Shaw's grave. One of them, it is believed, actually had the temerity to remove a stone and fling it into the Spey. But it did not remain long under water, since it was found in its rightful place the following morning, as though some occult power had replaced it. In any event, less than a week later, the body of the offending footman was recovered from the Spey, at a spot close to the Doune. Since that fatality, visitors to the old kirkyard of Rothiemurchus have comported themselves with great circumspection at the grave of Farquhar Shaw.

It is some years now since divine service was celebrated in the old Parish Church. In the days when the Grants were in possession and in residence, and all the inhabitants of the locality were their tenants or employees, it was well filled on Sundays. The communion-table it once contained was moved to the present Parish Church, down in the village of Inverdruie, which lies between the Doune and Aviemore. If you peep through the windows of the old church, you will see that the paint is peeling off the simple pulpit, where it is exposed to the sun's rays. At the very back of this old place of worship, which has no gallery, is the deserted Laird's Pew, its rose-coloured cushions worn in places and somewhat moth-eaten—just sufficiently deteriorated, when I peered at them through the window, to contribute an old-world touch to the setting.

Hard by the wooden gate admitting one to the churchyard, and overshadowed by firs and beeches, is a wooden shed housing a wheelbarrow, rakes, clippers, hoes, spades, and shovels, together with various other implements used in gardening, and in keeping down the rank weeds that soon spread riotously through an untended kirkyard. And in this shed a cobweb here, a cluster of crumpled leaves there, a scythe hanging by its blade from a rafter-beam, a withered leaf newly discarded from shedding tree, falling meticulously to earth by a door that is seldom closed.

\*　　\*　　\*　　\*　　\*

Just where the road diverts for Loch-an-Eilein is the high wall enclosing the tall oaks and beeches and pines which, in turn, hold in their embrace the large hollow containing the old garden of the Doune, with its sundial at the centre. A little beyond, and fenced off with wire-netting to restrain the Rothiemurchus rabbits from nibbling away all the flowers and vegetables, is the orchard of olden times, now standing in a wilderness of long grass and spreading broom, most of its fruit-trees too ancient for fruit-bearing in any quantity, their trunks and boughs bearded and hoary with grey tresses of lichen.

One dull day in October, when lingering through the garden after a heavy shower, and then up into the silent orchard, I felt this to be the saddest and most wistful place in all Rothiemurchus. The garden itself, although still fairly extensive, gave but scant evidence of the splendour that must have distinguished it in high summer. The few remaining flowers were drooping; and the searing fronds of riotous vegetables gave one a feeling of complete resignation, in the assurance that yet another spring would come, when everything would burst forth to life anew. A pair of tits hopped alertly about the tallest raspberry canes I ever beheld; and, high up among the tree-tops, a red squirrel passed along from plane-tree to beech, from beech-tree to oak, apparently effortless, and with an agility and swiftness instantly filling one with a sense of reverence and mystery—a sense of timelessness . . . of God. . . . No other thing seemed to be moving anywhere. Faint chirpings issued from the denser parts of the woody environs of the garden. But the birds emitting them remained unseen. No leaves stirred, except those on the slender twigs momentarily swayed by the nimble feet of the squirrel.

Most of the trees in the orchard, they told me at the Doune, now bear little fruit, although I counted a number of rosy, autumnal apples still clinging tenaciously to the boughs of some of them. But even yet, in time of spring, this orchard celebrates its pageantry of scented blossom, since fruit-trees continue to flower long after they are too old to bear fruit. In olden times a squad of gardeners was employed at the Doune; and it appeared astonishing how, to-day, one gardener and a boy manage to maintain this garden in such excellent order.

The beauty of this garden's setting completely removes the impression that it is a garden as much for culinary purposes as for flowers. The beetroot and the parsley, as essential to it as its flower-borders, recall those lines by Katharine Tynan:

> *When skies are blue and days are bright,*
> *The kitchen garden's my delight,*
> *Set round with rows of decent box,*
> *And blowsy girls of hollyhocks.*
>
> . . . . .
>
> *Sweet herbs in plenty, blue borage,*
> *And the delicious mint and sage,*
> *Rosemary, marjoram, and rue,*
> *And thyme to scent the winter through.*

\* \* \* \* \*

To glance along the pathway, sweeping down the centre of

the garden, between flower-beds, from the oaken bank on the east to the dark-green conifers on the west, must reveal the most glorious array of colour in June and July. Here no sound breaks upon the summer stillness, unless it be bird-song, or drone of bee, or perhaps the flutter of wood-pigeon the hue of lavender, high up among the dark interstices of the pines.

And, when I thought of the generations of children belonging to the Doune who, doubtless, romped in the orchard and gathered its bountiful harvest, I recalled what an old woman once said to me at Saddell as she gazed wistfully along the avenue leading to the old Castle. "And look at the avenue, too—yon lovely trees! It's just being allowed to go its own way. No one cares about it now; and it's sad to see the trees neglected. They must, indeed, be missing the voices of olden times."

$$\star \quad \star \quad \star \quad \star \quad \star$$

The Doune is not without its ghost and its brownie. Room 14—so I was informed by the manager of the Doune Hotel a year or so prior to the Second World War—is the Ghost Room. Of the brownie, nothing has been seen or heard for some years past. Tradition depones that, when the family flitted to the present building, one member of the household refused to quit the original site. That member was the brownie. During the night-time, faithful to the reputation of his species, he sallied forth to set the kitchen aright, washing up the dishes and tinkering the pots and pans. Long after the inmates of the Doune were abed, he could be heard at his tinkering, in return for "the cream-bowl duly set". But one night the laird, disturbed during sleep by the brownie's activities, rose in wrath. "Stop that din, and let decent folk sleep!" he shouted over the banister, whereupon the brownie deserted the Doune. When the servants came down in the morning, they found the hearth unswept, the dishes unwashed, the milk cogues unscoured, the leaking utensils unmended.

Then, Rothiemurchus is not without its tales of the rievers from Lochaber and elsewhere, who oftentimes invaded the quiet of its summer shielings. And the older residents still recount stories of the dreaded water-horse haunting Loch Pityoulish. Many of the tales of this neighbourhood concern the laird who, on account of his friendly relations with the MacGregors—the Clan Alpin—was known as MacAlpine. While playing at cards with Lord Lovat on one occasion, MacAlpine hesitated so long over his play that he exhausted Lovat's patience. " 'Deed, Lovat", he interposed, "truth to tell, I have a hand that puzzles me. *It's a knave between two kings—a hand you're better fitted to play yourself!*"

That there existed a bond of amity between MacAlpine and Rob Roy MacGregor is shown by a tale recounted in Rothiemurchus to this day. On the western confines of this ancient heritage The MacKintosh erected a mill, in order to work which he diverted a stream from running through the Rothiemurchus estate. Having received from Rob Roy an undertaking that, in time of stress, he could be called upon for help, MacAlpine wrote a strong letter of protest to The MacKintosh, who now hastened to retaliate by marching upon Rothiemurchus with fire and sword. As MacAlpine at this time was at variance with his own chief, and as Rob Roy lived so far away, he did not know where to turn for immediate assistance. But, while he sat brooding over his fire, with The MacKintosh and his men steadily closing in upon the Doune, he felt a firm hand on his shoulder. What was this but the hand of his friend and ally, Rob Roy?

"But where are your men, Rob?" asked MacAlpine, greatly agitated.

"Take you no heed o' that!" said Rob, as he called for his piper.

Rob then directed his piper to pace up and down in front of the Doune, playing *The MacGregors' Gathering*. As the piper continued to play, there appeared on the opposite bank of the Spey, at Kinrara, two MacGregors, and then three MacGregors, and then two MacGregors, and then three, until at length " a hundred and fifty of the prettiest men in Rob Roy's band were standing there, fully armed ". Now, the piper had been given instructions not to stop playing until the entire MacGregor force was visible; and we are told that the effort nearly burst him! As the MacGregors appeared in twos and threes, the Mac-Kintoshes, drawn up on the other bank of the river, slunk away in fours and fives, until the whole of their invading contingent had vanished.

In concluding this incident, Rob Roy is said to have addressed a letter to The MacKintosh at Moy Hall, warning him that, if ever it came to his knowledge that he, in any way whatsoever, was molesting the Laird of Rothiemurchus, or trespassing on his domain, Rob would not hesitate to lay waste his lands. In furtherance of this threat, Rob instructed MacAlpine to send for him on the slightest provocation from The MacKintosh.

"But it's a far cry to Balquhidder", Rob Roy observed; "and none in Rothiemurchus knows the way".

Thus it was that he left behind him, at the Doune, two young MacGregors, renowned for their fleetness of foot, to be sent forth by MacAlpine if ever he found himself in danger from The MacKintosh or, indeed, from any other person in the land.

At a later date, MacAlpine bestowed on one of the two MacGregors the farm of Alltdru, where he settled down and married, and duly begat several children. From generation to generation these MacGregors continued to live at Alltdru, until the time of Hamish (Jimmie) MacGregor, who died at the Doune Square in 1890. To me, a MacGregor, it was interesting to learn from the present laird, John Peter Grant, that, as a child, he used to be carried on the broad shoulders of old Jimmie MacGregor, the last surviving descendant in Rothiemurchus of the two clansmen left behind by my freebooting forebear.[1]

It was said of MacAlpine that he never retired for the night without praying for the wellbeing of two men. One of these was the Duke of Gordon, with whom he had had some amicable dealings: Rob Roy was the other.

Then, there is the story of the laird who, during the construction of the military roads through the Highlands after 'The Fifteen', began to find the visits of General Wade a little too frequent. So, one night, after the household was bedded, and he and Wade were left alone, the laird rose quietly, locked the door of the apartment in which they were, and proceeded to toast 'the King o'er the Water', passing his wine-glass over the water decanter while so doing. An insult as deliberate as this, Wade could not brook: never thereafter did he cast as much as his shadow on the threshold of the Doune.

---

[1] Incidentally, Sir Robert Hamilton Bruce Lockhart, whose mother was a Strathspey MacGregor, claims descent from one of the two MacGregors whom Rob Roy left behind at Rothiemurchus.

The last story of Rothiemurchus I propose giving you here is of more recent origin. A Scots padre, visiting a casualty clearing-station in Mesopotamia during the First World War, comforting Scottish soldiers where they were to be found, asked one of them where he had received his wound. The answer was precise enough: "*Three miles on the Rothiemurchus side of Bagdad!*"

In Rothiemurchus, where you may take the woodland path-ways among twigs and leaves and the cones and needles of pine-trees, each of the giant conifers has a personality of its own. I felt a contentment emanating from some divine dispensation creeping over me, as I stood a little distance away from the Doune one wet nightfall in October, sheltering under a plane-tree with leafage already so depleted that I would have been as dry had I stood out under the sky. Here I realized something of the resig-nation that outwits time, rendering of trifling account all the world's matters of urgency.

In winter-time the burns run garrulously through Rothie-murchus to augment the Spey which, each year, finds difficulty in keeping strictly to its own province. The snows, lying deep on the high-tops of the Cairngorms, and filling their clefts and corries, drive the deer down to the grassy plains for sustenance. From your bedroom window at the Doune, on a winter's morning, you may see a herd of deer grazing but a stone's-throw away.

Follow upstream from the Doune the track running along the elevated east bank of the Spey; and be on the lookout for the shy moorhen that so readily paddles out of sight where drooping boughs overhang the river's bank. This, surely, is one of the loveliest stretches of the incontinent Spey. If you tread quietly in this airt on a dull morning, you are certain to find a large flock of wild duck, or of wild geese, feeding under the banks.

And at candle-light one hears the hoot of ' the old woman of the night', invisible among the dark-set pines, marshalled by the western gable of the Doune like a phalanx of giants.

Much more might one write of Rothiemurchus if space allowed; but my advice to you is to read Elizabeth Grant's loving *Memoirs*.

# CHAPTER EIGHT

## COVENANTERS' CONVENTICLE—1666-1945

TO be reared in Auld Reekie without absorbing some knowledge of the Covenanters, however superficial, would indeed be an omission bordering on the incredible. What Scot, schooled in this ancient and venerable city, and having of necessity to learn something of the reigns of Charles the Second and James the Seventh, can have forgotten all he or she may once have been taught about the Pentland Rising, about Drumclog and Bothwell Brig, and about the Conventicles, those field-preachings to which the Cameronians—the hunted Covenanters—were obliged to resort? Surely, there can be no word more inseparably bound up with the Covenanters and their hazardous convenings and communings among the hills than the word, Conventicle: surely, for those of us with a background preponderately Scottish, there is enshrined in the name of Rullion Green a wisp of poignancy and sadness, such as the fervid Jacobite feels at merest whisper of Sheriffmuir or of Culloden.

Auld Reekie itself has much to remind one of the Cameronians and their Covenanting aspirations. I well remember the day my father, at all times ambitious that his offspring should be authoritatively informed on such matters, pointed out to me, in the National Museum of Antiquities, the flag borne by the Covenanters' army at Bothwell Brig, in 1679. If that exhibit brought vividly to mind those old defenders of the Presbyterian faith, which indeed it did, even more so did his taking me to Old Greyfriars', where, on a memorable Sabbath in 1638, the National Covenant was adopted and signed, and thereafter carried out to the kirkyard for the signatures of the multitude there assembled. The first to sign was Montrose—the very man who, subsequently, exerted himself so heroically, so fanatically, to defeat everything for which it stood. There cannot be many who, educated in Auld Reekie, do not recall in their Hume Brown the reproduction from William Hole's painting, showing the zealous populace gathered at Old Greyfriars', and appending its names to the Covenant as the parchment, whereon it was writ, lay spread upon the recumbent tombstone identified by tradition as that upon which this historic document was subscribed.

The ratification of the Covenant, with its solemn obligation to defend Presbyterianism, precipitated for Scotland half a century of woe, as Greyfriars' Kirkyard itself so truly testifies. There, in the oblong enclosure at the south-west corner, stands the Covenanters' Prison, where some twelve hundred of those rounded up by Royalist cavalry after Bothwell Brig were herded together for five wintry months, with no canopy but the cold, cloudy sky. In the most appalling misery, they were detained by a guard of soldiery charged, under pain of death, to allow no one to escape. Hundreds perished of exposure, and of brutal treatment received at the hands of those placed in authority over them : some few were given their freedom on swearing to a bond never again to take up arms against the King, or without his permission : some four hundred declined this avenue of release, " not accepting deliverance, that they might obtain a better resurrection " : some two hundred and sixty perished, when the vessel transporting them from Leith to the Barbadoes slave plantations was wrecked off the Orkneys, and only forty of their number were saved.

Few persecutions in the cruel history of mankind were pursued with greater ruthlessness, which explains the Martyrs' Monument erected in 1771 in the north-east corner of this same kirkyard, the most historical and celebrated place of burial in Scotland, excepting not even Iona.

The Martyrs' Monument bears the following inscription :

> " Halt, passenger! take heed what you do see—
> This tomb doth show for what some men did die :
> Here lies interred the dust of those who stood
> 'Gainst perjury, resisting unto blood ;
> Adhering to the covenants and laws,
> Establishing the same ; which was the cause
> Their lives were sacrificed unto the lust
> Of prelatists abjured ; though here their dust
> Lies mix't with murderers, and other crew,
> Whom justice justly did to death pursue.
> But, as for them no cause was to be found
> Worthy of death ; but only they were found
> Constant and steadfast, zealous, witnessing
> For the prerogatives of Christ, their King ;

*Which truths were sealed by famous Guthrie's head,*
*And all along to Mr. Renwick's blood.*
*They did endure the wrath of enemies:*
*Reproaches, torment, death, and injuries.*
*But yet they're those who from such troubles came,*
*And now triumph in glory with the Lamb!*

"*From May 27, 1661, that the most noble Marquis of Argyle was beheaded, to the 17th February, 1688, that Mr. James Renwick suffered, were one way or other murdered and destroyed for the same cause about eighteen thousand, of whom were executed at Edinburgh about a hundred of noblemen and gentlemen, ministers and others—noble martyrs for Jesus Christ. The most of them lie here.*"

Indeed, they do, "mix't with murderers and other crew", since in olden times this part of Old Greyfriars' Kirkyard was given over to the burial of murderers and other executed malefactors.

Here also, at Greyfriars', as if in satirical contrast, is the mausoleum of Sir George MacKenzie of Rosehaugh, founder of the Advocates' Library. Because of the severity with which, as King's Advocate for Scotland, he prosecuted the Covenanters, he is better known to us as Bluidy MacKenzie.

\* \* \* \* \*

Roughly eight miles to the south of Auld Reekie, on the eastern slope of Turnhouse Hill, and at a spot called Rullion Green, there was fought, in 1666, the battle in which the Covenanters, led by Colonel James Wallace,[1] were routed by the King's troops under General Sir Thomas Dalyell (or Dalziel) of The Binns, their commander-in-chief in Scotland. Dalziel, who refused to cut his beard after the execution of Charles the First, had seen service in

---

[1] While these pages were in press, I received from a Miss Daphne Wallace (*b.* 1924) living at Chippenham, a letter she wrote me after reading in *Auld Reekie : Portrait of a Lowland Boyhood* my brief references to Rullion Green, and to her forebear, Colonel James Wallace, of Auchens. Daphne's family tree, a copy of which she sends me, shows her to be a direct lineal descendant of the Covenanting Colonel. He was her great-great-great-great-great-grandfather.

"I thought you might be interested to learn what became of him after the Battle of Rullion Green", she writes, "if you do not already know. He fled to Holland. How long he stayed there, history does not seem to relate. But some old papers suggest he joined a continental army, and fought there, though we have no definite proof of this. From Holland he went to Ireland, with a high price on his head, because of his Scottish activities. He settled near Lough Bric-land ('lake of the speckled fish') in Co. Down. There he lived in retirement, concealing his identity even from his children. His seal was found among his possessions by his son after his death, and also the details of his origin.

"We have in the family his two broadswords with Andrea Ferrara blades, one of which he is reputed to have used at Rullion Green. These swords were brought by him to Holland from Scotland. I have no actual proof of this, but every reason to believe it to be true."

Russia and in Poland, and had taken part in expeditions against Turk and Tartar. In 1681 he raised the Scots Greys.[1]

Over fifty Covenanters are said to have been killed at Rullion Green. Several of those who escaped with their lives, and not a few of whom had been wounded, were brought in afterwards by the country people; and it is believed that, in addition to these, numbers of others were shot or slain while in flight from the scene of their disaster, and were buried in neighbouring kirkyards. Many are said to lie at Penicuik, and many more in the kirkyard at Glencorse. In the kirk-session records of the former one finds the following minute : "*Dec., 9th, 1666. Disbursed to John Brown belman for making westlandmen's graves 3s. 4d.*"

Rullion Green was fought on the 28th of November of that year.

For a day and a night, the vanquished Covenanters lay un-buried, and, according to Colonel Wallace, were stripped of their apparel "by the soldiers and the barbarians of Lothian, as if the victory had been gotten over the Turks ; but the godly women of Edinburgh came out on the morrow with winding sheets, and buried them ".

On the Pentland hillside at Rullion Green, by the fringe of a sparse woodland overlooking the battlefield, with the rich tilth

---

[1] In 1946 the historic House of The Binns, situated near Linlithgow, was handed over to the National Trust for Scotland by Mrs. Eleanor Dalyell of The Binns, when the ancient and symbolic ceremony of earth and stone was observed. Mrs. Dalyell's young son, who is now at Eton, cut a bit of turf, and broke a fragment of stone from the wall. These he handed to his mother, who, in turn, handed them to the Earl of Wemyss, saying as she did so : " With this earth and stone I give you sasine of The Binns on behalf of the National Trust for Scotland." The Earl, in accepting them, responded in like formula.

Mrs. Dalyell, after expressing herself in sympathy with the aims and purposes of the Trust, said that she and her husband and son were desirous that the house, so rich in legends and so long associated with the historic family of Dalyell of The Binns, should be pre-served as it stood, in all time coming, for the benefit and enjoyment of the nation. That this might be rendered possible, an endowment in land and in money had also been made.

Under the terms of the Trust's charter, Mrs. Dalyell reserves the sole right to use the territorial title, ' of The Binns ' ; to fly, when resident there, the armorial banner of Dalyell of The Binns ; to hold the Baron Court in the Laigh Hall ; and to appoint the Baron Bailie and the Baron Officer. She also reserves the right to the hidden treasure of The Binns, if ever it should be found.

The house, which is now open to the public on Saturdays, when visitors are taken round by the Baron Officer, contains several historic portraits and relics. Many of the latter belonged to General Tam Dalyell, as he is known to Scottish history—the very Tam who defeated the Covenanters at Rullion Green. Among these are his Bible, sword, spurs, riding boots, camp spoon, dagger, and comb. It was with this comb that General Tam combed the beard he swore he would never cut, until the King came into his own again.

of East Lothian stretching beyond, as far as the foothills of the Lammermuirs, you will discover the Martyrs' Tomb. There, where the hill-wind goes a-sighing through pines and beeches, and in autumn hurries the seared and curling leaves along the numerous sheep-tracks intersecting this sequestered spot, were interred most of the slain Covenanters. Some doubt seems to exist as to who raised the stone on the fringe of the wood; but perhaps some of my readers may be able to tell us.

On one side of this stone we read: *"Here and near to this place lyes the Reverend Mr. John crookshank and Mr. Andrew m'cormack ministers of the Gospels and about fifty other True covenanted presbyterians who were killed in this place in their own Inocent self defence and defence of the covenanted work of Reformation By Thomas Dalzeel of Bins upon the 28 of november 1666 Rev XII 11 Erected September 28, 1738."*

On turning to the passage alluded to, we find one of the texts from which the Covenanters derived solace during the Killing Time, and upon which, even at the present day, the clergy ministering to their descendants frequently base their sermons. Indeed, this text appears on several of the Covenanters' memorials —*"And they overcame him by the Blood of the Lamb, and by the word of their testimony; and they loved not their lives unto the death."*

And what of the other side of the stone by the copse's fringe, among the sheep-tracks at Rullion Green?

> *A cloud of witnesses lyes here,*
> *Who for Christ's interest did appear,*
> *For to restore true Liberty*
> *Overturned then by Tyrrany*
> *And by Proud Prelats who did rage*
> *Against the Lord's own heritage.*
> *They sacrificed were for the Laws*
> *Of Christ their King, his noble cause.*
> *These heroes fought with great renown,*
> *By falling got the Martyr's Crown.*

Even since that fateful day in the fall of 1666, much of this Pentland Country would seem to have remained sacred to the memory of the Covenanters. Here and there about it, from time to time, were found the remains of some fugitive from Rullion Green. Many of the wounded are believed to have succumbed in our Pentland bogs, when endeavouring to reach the West Land, whence most of them had come—Lanarkshire, or Ayrshire, or perhaps distant Galloway—and where, among the remote hills, the Covenanters, for the most part, held their Conventicles in defiance, until the dragoons cruelly harassed them, putting them to the sword or to flight.

The plough of a certain John Gill, who was the first to till the soil at Rullion Green after the Revolution of 1688, turned up the bones of many a martyr. These were reverently collected, and buried together on the hillside yonder, where moulders the dust of the true covenanted Presbyterians.

*　　*　　*　　*　　*

Among the best known of the Covenanters' graves about the Pentland Hills is that of the nameless fugitive who died at Oaken Bush the day after Rullion Green, and was buried by Adam Sanderson, of Blackhill, a small farm that once existed near Dunsyre, in Lanarkshire. The grave is marked by a stone standing on the moorland slope of the hill known as the Black Law. Tradition has it that a Covenanter, sorely wounded, and striving to reach Ayrshire, came to Adam Sanderson's threshold in the dead of night, and asked that he might be given some temporary relief. He refused to tarry long, however, expressing the fear that his so doing might endanger those upon whose mercy he had cast himself. Early the following day, Sanderson set out with him on the first stage of his hopeless journey homeward. Soon his strength failed him; and he lay down to die. "Bury me in sight of the Ayrshire hills!" was his dying request. So Sanderson carried his corpse from Oaken Bush to the heathery spot on the slope of the Black Law, where stands the tombstone erected to his memory, many years later, and wherefrom, on a clear day, one gets a glimpse of his native Ayrshire, some twenty miles afar.

*　　*　　*　　*　　*

One Sunday afternoon in June, some thirty years ago or thereabouts, during my schoolhood in Edinburgh, I happened to be descending Turnhouse Hill when my ear caught the strains of metrical psalm-singing, as though a vast congregation were

157

worshipping in the open. In a setting impressed upon one through the pages of Hume Brown, I instantly thought of the Covenanters, and of the Conventicles they had held among these very hills. On reaching the road at Flotterstane Brig, I was astonished to find, on the grassy patch I now know to be Flotterstane Haugh Field, a large gathering assembled for public worship in true Covenanter fashion. With the aid of a Precentor, it was singing, to the tune, *Crimond*, the metrical version of the 23rd Psalm:

> *The Lord's my shepherd, I'll not want.*
> *He makes me down to lie*
> *In pastures green: he leadeth me*
> *The quiet waters by.*
>
> .    .    .    .    .
>
> *Goodness and mercy all my life*
> *Shall surely follow me:*
> *And in God's house for evermore*
> *My dwelling-place shall be.*

Not since the days of my Highland childhood, when, in the summer-time, we celebrated our Presbyterian Communion in the open air, had I heard and seen anything on the Sabbath quite so reminiscent of the Covenanters.

Under the auspices of the Reformed Presbyterian Church at Loanhead, and for many years now, it has been customary to hold, in the Preaching Field at Flotterstane, almost within earshot of Rullion Green, a memorial service, after the manner of the Covenanters' Conventicles. It was upon one such annual service I had come, unwittingly, that Sabbath afternoon in June. Though, as you may remember, the battle was fought in November, June was the month adopted for this commemoration, because one could be assured of better weather then, and consequently of an encouraging attendance, not only from Edinburgh itself, but also from several of the towns, villages, and isolated homesteads of the Lothians.

\*    \*    \*    \*    \*

Now we come to 1945.

When in Auld Reekie during the autumn of that year, I happened one day to see in a local newspaper a public notice intimating that, on the following Sunday afternoon, the annual service, commemorating the Covenanters' stand at Rullion Green, was to be held once more at the same spot, and under the same auspices. This service had been in abeyance during the war years. In the ordinary course of events, it would have been arranged for the month of June; but hostilities did not cease in time to make this possible. However, by those anxious to re-institute this quaint reminder of so arduous and cruel an episode in Scotland's history, it was thought that the coming of peace afforded the opportunity for its immediate revival.

To this service—to this Covenanters' Conventicle, as one might appropriately describe it—I duly betook myself, somewhat circuitously. A Sabbath morning of mellowing sunshine urged me to take to the hills in the manner sought by those of Auld Reekie who cherish their Pentland background. The service, due to begin at 3 p.m., had just begun as I reached Flotterstane by way of the summit of Carnethy, the shoulder of Turnhouse Hill, and Rullion Green itself. Had this Conventicle been held on the battlefield, my descent from these loftier regions would have brought me to the scene in good time. There is something to be said for the view that it should have been held on the actual site of the battle—perhaps, up at the Martyrs' Tomb. Yet, this would prove disadvantageous to many of the older people who have attended it regularly for years. Flotterstane Haugh Field is reasonably accessible, since it lies but a stone's-throw from the highway linking Edinburgh with the south, by way of Carlops, West Linton, and Biggar—a situation, the convenience of which you will appreciate the more when I tell you that, among those attending the Conventicle this autumn, was an octogenarian Covenanter known throughout the Pentlands as Bob Campbell. At the age of eleven, Bob was taken to his first Rullion Green Conventicle by his aunt, a firm believer in the Covenanters and their cause. He has been present at every Conventicle since.

Bob began life as grave-digger and hedger at Old Pentland, where lie buried many of the earliest Covenanters and their descendants. Later, he farmed at Ferniehaugh, a wild Pentland spot between Dolphinton and Medwinhead. Now he lives in retirement at Slipperfield, not far from West Linton, whence a bus conveys him and his Covenanting cronies to the memorial service. Among the hundreds gathered together at Flotterstane

Haugh Field each year are several quite old people—staunch adherents of the Presbyterian faith as originally covenanted.

\*　\*　\*　\*　\*

Nothing but the metrical Psalms are sung at this Conventicle, they being the sole 'praise' permitted in the Reformed Presbyterian Church. They are sung unaccompanied, but with the aid of a Precentor who 'sings the line' in the old style, after he has consulted his tuning-fork. Even the Metrical Paraphrases, which are known to so many Scots, and are to be found at the back of their Bibles, are excluded. Anything in the nature of a hymn, of course, would be impossible to imagine at such a service, which at all times is conducted in the austerest and simplest fashion. From the ease and gusto with which nearly everyone at this Conventicle sang the Metrical Psalms, with but brief and occasional reference to the song-sheet distributed among the assembly, it was evident that the vast majority of those present were Scots Presbyterians of one denomination or another.

It was truly appropriate on this occasion that the minister conducting the service should have chosen as the complementary texts from which he preached, firstly, the verse from Revelation denoted at the Martyrs' Tomb, and, secondly, those memorable verses with which the eleventh chapter of Hebrews concludes:

*And others had trial of cruel mockings and scourgings, yea, moreover of bonds and imprisonment:*

*They were stoned, they were sawn asunder, were tempted, were slain with the sword: they wandered about in sheepskins and goatskins; being destitute, afflicted, tormented;*

*(Of whom the world was not worthy:) they wandered in deserts, and in mountains, and in dens and caves of the earth.*

*And these all, having obtained a good report through faith, received not the promise:*

*God having provided some better thing for us, that they without us should not be made perfect.*

Thus it was with many who found graves among the lonely hills, nearly three centuries ago. They kept the faith, and died for Scotland's Covenanted Cause. One could not hear these scriptural words, sent forth upon the autumn air at Flotterstane, without recalling not merely the names of the warriors of whom we know—Cameron, Cargill, Guthrie, Hislop, MacKail, Peden, Renwick, and the rest—but also the steadfastness of the *nameless* folk—those Unknown Warriors—who, likewise, perished for the Covenants. Nameless they are, indeed; and nameless they must needs remain. Yet, an Edinburgh know-all declared at this Conventicle that, after much research, he was now in a position to tell us the name of him whom Adam Sanderson comforted, and to whose memory was erected the stone on the slopes of the Black Law, in view of the Ayrshire Hills. Carfin, he declared, was the name of this Covenanter hitherto nameless. But what of it? Would any useful purpose be served by our making investigations such as might disclose the name of the Unknown Warrior buried at Westminster Abbey?

It was interesting that the Bible used on this occasion, as at previous Conventicles held in Flotterstane Haugh Field, was an old, tattered, eighteenth-century one that, for generations, was in the Sanderson family. At present it belongs to Miss Jean McMorran, who resides at the little Midlothian town of Bonny-rigg, and who lends it each year. Miss McMorran inherited it from her uncle, George Sanderson, a descendant of the very Adam Sanderson who succoured the nameless Covenanter, and buried him as he had desired. For centuries, and, in fact, until a few years ago, there were many Sandersons dwelling about Dun-syre, Dykefoot, Blackhill, and Medwinhead. To-day, in these Pentland places, there is none of the name to be found.

$$\ast \quad \ast \quad \ast \quad \ast \quad \ast$$

A word or two, in conclusion, about the Reformed Presby-terian Church.

The Cameronians, as many of the Scottish Covenanters were called, felt they could not join the Revolution Church of Scotland, brought into being in 1690, under the government of William of Orange, for they held that, although it was Presbyterian in its order, it ignored the Covenants, and accepted a measure of State interference in spiritual matters. It admitted the Crown's right to dissolve Church assemblies, for instance; and it accepted the system of patronage. For sixteen years, the dissenting Cove-nanters maintained their own Societies for worship and religious correspondence. By 1706 there existed in Scotland twenty such Societies, with a membership of roughly seven thousand. In 1743 there was constituted the Reformed Presbytery, whereafter the Church increased its membership so appreciably that in 1810 the Presbytery was divided regionally into a Northern, Eastern, and Southern Presbytery. A year later, these three Presbyteries convened as the first Synod of the Reformed Presbyterian Church of Scotland. That year, moreover, the Irish and the North American Reformed Presbyterian Churches—offshoots of the Scottish—were strong enough to set up their own first Synods. To-day there are between thirty and forty of their congregations in Ireland, and over a hundred in America.

In Scotland this religious body was divided, in 1863, over the question of the parliamentary franchise. A majority supported the view that the Synod should dispense with the rule of political dissent, thus abandoning the basis of the Covenants, and sharing responsibility for national sins which, notwithstanding, it still exposed and condemned. The minority stood its ground, resolutely declining to share in the responsibility of elected law-makers. On the contrary, it maintained, at a Synod of its own, the Reformed Presbyterian pledge not to countenance political systems which, in its view, ignored the primary rights of Christ Jesus as King of the world's nations.

Finally, in 1876, the majority of the Reformed Presbyterian Church united with the Free Church of Scotland. The remnant eight congregations still existing north of the Tweed are the survival of the minority of 1863. As I have said, the congregation at Loanhead, in Midlothian, makes itself responsible for the Rullion Green Conventicle. Its minister conducts the service; and its precentor and choir lead the 'praise'.

Even yet, the members of this austere body, true to the Covenanters' testimony, abstain from participation in parliamentary and other elections, as a protest against the failure of the constitution to regard Christian standards as paramount in the matter of the nation's government.

The Church's discipline has always been rigid. Mr. James Campbell, its Precentor at Loanhead, told me the other day that, during Mr. Gladstone's parliamentary campaign in North Midlothian, and as the kirk-session records show, his agèd grandfather,

Stone marking the grave of an Unknown Covenanter on the
moorland slopes of the Black Law

Eighteenth-century Bible used at the annual Covenanters' Conventicle at Flotterstane, near Rullion Green

3

In Old Greyfriars' Kirkyard,
Edinburgh.

1 The Martyrs' Monument
2 The Covenanter's Prison
3 Bluidy MacKenzie's Tomb

Looking eastward over Rullion Green from Turnhouse Hill, toward Flotterstane, in the middle-distance. Beyond lie the rich farmlands of East Lothian, with the Moorfoot Hills vaguely seen on the skyline

Looking northward across Rullion Green to Castlelaw

*Above :* The Martyrs' Tomb at Rullion Green

*Below :* Ruins of Adam Sanderson's home at Blackhill, near
Medwinhead, in Lanarkshire

who lived at Bonnyrigg and walked every Sunday to service at Loanhead, was forcibly carried off by four men to the polling-booth, that he might be compelled to record his vote. This he did, under duress, with the result that he was haled before the session, and rebuked for his grave deflection. He promised he would never vote again, under any circumstances.

The same kirk-session records disclose that in the year, 1875, a member of the congregation was convicted on a charge of reset. A little later, he was ordered to compear before the session, to be deprived of all the privileges of church membership—communion, baptism, marriage, burial—for eighteen months. At the end of that period, the delinquent was directed to come before the kirk-session again, in order that it might ascertain whether he realized the seriousness of the offence he had committed, and was sufficiently penitent to justify his being re-admitted to membership. He was duly reinstated.

How does so small a church exist? you may ask. How does it manage, financially? How does it maintain the minimum stipend? The answer to such questions is to be found in the loyalty of its members, both as regards the regularity of their attendance at worship, and their extreme generosity where the welfare of their Church is concerned.

These are the Presbyterians of the Reformed Church, who, with due reverence for things long held precious in memory, still keep tryst at Rullion Green, as did their Covenanting forebears, nearly three hundred years ago.